Fodor's 91

Jamaica

Gary Diedrichs

D1176738

FODOR'S TRAVEL PUBLICATIONS, INC.
New York & London

ISBN 0–679–01921–9

Fodor's Jamaica

Editor: Andrew E. Beresky
Editorial Contributor: Sandra Hart
Drawings: Ted Burwell, Michael Kaplan
Maps: Mark Stein Studios
Cover Photograph: Paul Barton

Cover Design: Vignelli Associates

SPECIAL SALES

Fodor's Travel Publications are available at special discounts for bulk purchases
(100 copies or more) for sales promotions or premiums. Special editions, including personalized covers, excerpts of existing guides, and corporate imprints, can
be created in large quantities for special needs. For more information, write to
Special Marketing, Fodor's Travel Publications, 201 East 50th Street, New
York, NY 10022. Inquiries from the United Kingdom should be sent to Fodor's
Travel Publications, 20 Vauxhall Bridge Road, London SW1V 25A.

MANUFACTURED IN THE UNITED STATES OF AMERICA
10   9   8   7   6   5   4   3   2   1

Contents

Maps and Plans

Foreword

Visitors to Jamaica will naturally expect to find inviting stretches of sand, warm tropical breezes, and an unhurried lifestyle. What they are often surprised to find, however, is that there is more to Jamaica than just soft, white beaches. Jamaica possesses a rich history and colorful culture that the island and her people are happy to share with visitors.

This guide is designed to help the traveler navigate the multitude of cultural, historical, and recreational diversions that Jamaica offers. Our writers have attempted to seek out the best tours, the most spectacular sunsets, and the most exciting nightlife and present them to you for easy reference, so the days you spend in Jamaica can become warm memories for a lifetime.

While every care has been taken to assure the accuracy of the information in this guide, the passage of time will always bring change, and consequently the publisher cannot accept responsibility for errors that may occur.

All prices and opening times quoted here are based on information available to us at press time. Hours and admission fees may change, however, and the prudent traveler will avoid inconvenience by calling ahead.

Fodor's wants to hear about your travel experiences, both pleasant and unpleasant. When a hotel or restaurant fails to live up to its billing, let us know and we will investigate the complaint and revise our entries where the facts warrant it.

Send your letters to the editors of Fodor's Travel Publications, 201 E. 50th Street, New York, NY 10022.

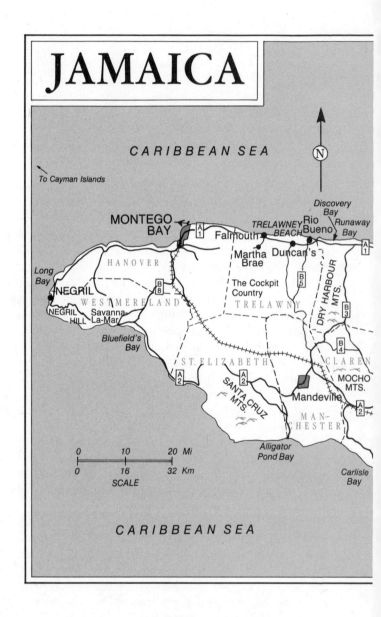

JAMAICA

CARIBBEAN SEA

N

To Cayman Islands

Discovery
Bay

MONTEGO
BAY

TRELAWNEY
BEACH

Rio
Bueno

Runaway
Bay

A
1

Falmouth

Duncan's

A
1

Martha
Brae

HANOVER

Long
Bay

NEGRIL

B
8

The Cockpit
Country

B
5

DRY HARBOUR MTS.

B
3

WESTMERELAND

TRELAWNY

NEGRIL
HILL

Savanna-
La-Mar

B
4

Bluefield's
Bay

CLAREN

ST. ELIZABETH

A
2

A
2

MOCHO
MTS.

SANTA CRUZ
MTS.

Mandeville

A
2

MAN-
CHESTER

0   10   20 Mi

0   16   32 Km

SCALE

Alligator
Pond Bay

Carlisle
Bay

CARIBBEAN SEA

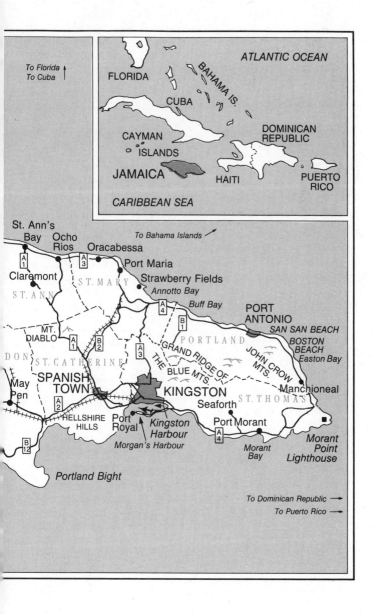

Introduction

"No problem, *mon*. . ." Wherever you venture on the island of Jamaica, whatever you ask, the answer is the same. It can be done. Not to worry. Life is to be enjoyed. There is a devotion to *living* here. It is an intense devotion, all-encompassing, and yet no big deal. If you feel like singing, you sing; if you feel like dancing, you dance. No problem, *mon*.

It is difficult, if not impossible, not to join the party. But why resist? The first sight of, say, the young MBA from Chicago, her blond hair newly braided into tight corn rows, swaying to a joyous reggae beat drifting across a splendid expanse of white, powdery sand strikes you as incongruous. You watch as others join in: the lawyer from New York, his T-shirt reading, NO PROBLEM; the honeymooning couple from Atlanta. Soon it's an impromptu celebration.

Off to one side, the tall Jamaican, his dreadlocks tucked into a green-and-black woolen cap, is grinning approval and swaying, too. Now you begin to believe that the sweet life in Jamaica really is no problem, *mon*.

Even in a Caribbean dotted with islands of beauty and magic, there is something special about Jamaica. Its beauty, its magic, are expressed in so many different ways.

See them, for example, in the diversity of the Jamaican

scenery, one of the richest and most varied in the world
. . . From the seven miles of uninterrupted sand along
Negril Beach and those sunny playgrounds of the north
shore, Montego Bay and Ocho Rios, to the astonishing
eagle's eye views and alpine cool of the Blue Mountains or
the high country around the inland town of Mandeville
. . . From the low, dark-green, shrimp-filled marshlands
edging the Black River to the pock-marked limestone crags
of the mysterious Cockpit Country . . . From the capital city
of Kingston, chaotic yet mesmerizing, to the calm of the
fishing village of Port Antonio.

See them in Jamaica's diverse population. "Out of
Many, One People"—so goes the national motto. The nation's 2.3 million citizens are a piquant and pleasing mix of
African, European, East Indian, and Chinese. Along the
highways, in the villages and towns, your mind can't help
but snap unending freeze frames, mental snapshots to sum-
mon this time long after you have come and gone: the
school children, so fresh in their neatly pressed uniforms,
waving exuberantly as you pass; the weekend cricketers
dressed all in white on the long green lawn; the shy young
women, gossiping quietly to each other as they tend to the
shops behind Kingston's famous Devon House.

And there's the enthusiasm of Danny Melville, creator
of Chukka Cove at St. Ann's Bay, who has developed 50
acres of land into the finest equestrian and polo center in
the Caribbean. He talks excitedly of the annual arrival of
Captain Mark Philips, who takes a break from his royal
duties in England to teach show jumping and dressage to
anyone who cares to attend. Or the woolly-headed man
called Prince Julie, displaying his handwoven hammocks by
the Negril roadside, who invites you to take a heady whiff
of his lima-bean soup that bubbles over an open fire. Or the
man "come down from deh mountin" who sells you the
heavy walking stick he carved from ironwood. Or the white-
gloved waiter named James who chases a peacock out of his
path as he delivers a breakfast tray at Trident Villas in Port
Antonio.

There's also the music, of course: folk ballads, work
songs, revivalist hymns; mento, Jamaica's folk music—sensuous, irresistible; reggae, influenced by the Rastafarian
religious cult, and alive with the memory of Bob Marley and

carried on today by son Ziggy Marley, Dennis Brown, Jimmy Cliff, Greg Isaacs, and others.

The food is colorful and pungent; the drink, ubiquitous rum, Red Stripe beer, as well as nonalcoholic thirst quenchers in exotic flavors like soursop, tamarind, sorrel, and almost everywhere, late afternoon tea.

The flora and fauna? Bougainvillea, hibiscus, oleander, poinsettia, ackee, breadfruit, cassia, guangao, logwood, naseberry, bananas, sugar cane, pimento, coffee; the whistling frog, mongoose, hummingbird, and gloriously plumed doctor bird.

The first human inhabitants, the Arawak Indians, called the island Xaymaca, meaning Land of Wood and Water. It is also a land rich in bauxite—Jamaica is the world's third largest producer of this mineral that is smelted into aluminum—as well as limestone, marble, alabaster, and sandstone. In area it is 4,411 square miles, third largest in the Caribbean. At its longest, Jamaica stretches 144 miles; at its widest, 52 miles. From its central backbone of mountains running east to west—the Blue Mountain Peak rises 7,402 feet above the sea—waterfalls, springs, rivers, and streams flow to the fertile plains and beaches which circle the island.

The Arawak Indians had inhabited the island for nearly five centuries before Christopher Columbus arrived in 1494. The Arawaks were a gentle tribe of hunters and fishermen, known to farm occasionally and celebrate numerous festivals. The arrival of the Spanish, however, signaled the extinction of the Arawaks. The Indians were forced into hard labor, which obliterated the tribe within 50 years.

Once they had Jamaica to themselves, the Spanish seemed to decide they didn't really want it anyway. Their searches turned up no quick-profit precious metals, so they let the island fester in poverty for 161 years. In 1655, British troops appeared in Kingston harbor. The Spanish were only too happy to flee.

The next three centuries under English rule provided Jamaica with both the genteel underpinnings of its present life and the rousing pirate tradition that enlivens this entire period of Caribbean history. British buccaneer Henry Morgan counted Jamaica's governor as one of his closest friends and enjoyed the protection of His Majesty's government whenever he visited the island. The notorious Port Royal prospered on a spit of land across the harbor from present-day Kingston precisely because it served so many lawless interests. It continued to serve them right up until June 7, 1692, when an earthquake tilted two thirds of Port Royal into the sea and a tidal wave wiped out whatever was left.

The eighteenth century was one of great prosperity in Jamaica, thanks to the sugar barons and their British-style plantations. The island was the world's largest sugar-producing colony until, as with cotton in the American South, sugar proved less profitable when slavery was abolished in 1838.

By the mid 1900s, a "national identity" had supplanted a British one in the hearts and minds of Jamaicans. This new identity was given official recognition on August 6, 1962, when Jamaica became an independent nation with only loose ties to the Commonwealth.

This is a country fraught with both promise and poverty. Economic and political problems disrupted the norm in the 1970s; and as recently as 1985 there were disturbances in Kingston following a steep hike in the price of gasoline.

Yet the hope of better days seems more than illusory. The government has worked hard to promote tourism as a primary building block for the future—even to the point of urging its people to smile more. In traditional Jamaica, a smile is a sign of genuine friendship, something to be earned, rather than a casual form of greeting. At heart, most Jamaicans are old-fashioned and like a show of good manners. When you need assistance, such words as good morning and thanks—"howdy" and "tenky"—will work wonders.

In the aftermath of 1988's Hurricane Gilbert, the island is more closely bound to tourism than ever before. Nearly 500 years after Christopher Columbus arrived, Jamaicans have finally committed themselves wholeheartedly to the tourist trade. The hurricane, in a sense, decided destiny for them. Though Gilbert ransacked both the agricultural and livestock-producing areas on the island, the resort-rich North Coast was left largely untouched, and tourism became a primary concern for the nation's financial survival.

General Information

The weather in Jamaica? Well, *almost* no problem. Though a tropical country, Jamaica does have variations in climate, depending on where you are and the time of year. From December to April, daytime temperatures hover between 70 and 80 degrees; in Kingston, though, the thermometer may well top 90 degrees. Summer readings are usually in the high 80s to low 90s. Trade winds from the northeast and mountain breezes keep things pleasant along the coast (by day, the so-called "doctor's breeze" blows in from the sea, by night the "undertaker's breeze" blows back to the sea). Year-round, though, the higher you go, the cooler it gets. Mandeville, perched in the cool hills of Manchester, as well as the coffee plantations of the Blue Mountains, can be downright refreshing, even crisp—as daytime temperatures dip at least 10 degrees below coastal levels.

   In late spring (May through early June) and autumn (October to early November), daily rain showers are common; they're typically brief, cleansing, and followed by a drying sun. Port Antonio, on the lush northeast coast, sees the most frequent shower activity, but these, too, are usually very little problem: the air dampens under cover of darkness and early morning, but by 11 A.M. another glorious day has begun.

In short, you can be reasonably confident that, apart from the possibility of a few raindrops falling on your head plus their accompanying cloud cover, your stay will not be marred by bad weather. Indeed, perfect beach weather is the most likely forecast. When, then, should you go? If cost and crowds are no impediment, anytime will do. Be advised, however, that mid-December to Easter is peak tourist season—Christmas and New Year's in particular. Hotel rooms are at their most scarce, prices their highest, and all the tourist attractions their most crowded. Reservations several months in advance are always a good idea. During peak periods, they are virtually essential.

One caveat: The active hurricane season runs from mid-August through mid-October.

PHONING JAMAICA

The area code for Jamaica is 809; from the United States you dial 1–809 and then the local number. If you call from 7 A.M. to 4 P.M., your local time, rates are surprisingly reasonable. Be sure to ask that a written confirmation of hotel accommodations be mailed.

When making reservations or inquiries by phone from home, always check first with the "800" information operator (dial 800–555–1212) to see if a toll-free number is available for where you're calling. Many of the major Jamaican hotels offer 800 numbers these days.

Within the country, phone service is maddening: a new "improved" system, ICAS, installed in the late 1980s, now makes it almost impossible to reach numbers in the next town when dialing within Jamaica. Overseas calls are better, but that won't help when you are trying to make a dinner reservation. So be sure to make arrangements for accommodations before arrival.

Emergency numbers for the entire island: Police and Air-Sea Rescue is 119; fire department and ambulance, 110.

JAMAICA TIME

When it's noon in Washington, D.C., it's also noon in the Jamaican capital of Kingston—and all of this island nation. Except in summertime. Jamaican clocks are set on Eastern standard time year-round; daylight-saving time is not observed.

So much for actual time. What about the Jamaican *sense* of time? Expect—and learn to savor—a slower pace, a Caribbean casualness regarding timetables and appointed hours. Things get done, but why rush? "Soon come," as the islanders say. Translation: relax and enjoy.

THE YEAR IN JAMAICA

Banks and most stores are closed on New Year's Day, Ash Wednesday, Good Friday, Easter Monday, Labour Day (May 23), National Heroes Day (third Monday in October), Christmas, and Boxing Day (December 26).

. Toward the end of January into early February, a chance to witness first-class polo is yours at the annual Chukka Cove Cup competition in Ocho Rios; the Jamaica Open (AJPA) Polo Tournament is held in mid-March; and the annual Red Stripe International Polo Tournament is held in April. Every Thursday and most weekends, there's polo of some sort going on at Chukka.

Early March sees Manchester Golf Week in Mandeville, the island's oldest golf tournament, with more than a half-century of tradition behind it. A few weeks later the Miami-to-Montego Bay Yacht Race, begun in 1961, brings excitement and a round of social events. The largest flower show in the Caribbean, well over an acre of flora, is hosted by the Jamaica Horticultural Society in Kingston toward the end of April.

If you're in Kingston in early May, the manicured lawns of King's House—official residence of Jamaica's Governor General—are the site of Her Excellency's May Day Charities, a popular yearly event that includes food, music, and dance. Later in the month, Ocho Rios hosts the Jamaica International Marlin Tournament and the Trelawny Carnival livens up the town of Falmouth with a parade and well-known Caribbean musicians in concert.

August is a month for parades, music, costume pageants, and all the pomp that goes into celebration of the anniversary of Jamaica's birth as a sovereign nation on August 6th, 1962. Partying is most intense in the capital of Kingston, but the whole country joins in. Near month's end Montego Bay is overrun by the thousands who gather from the world over for the five days of the internationally acclaimed Reggae Sunsplash concerts. Around this same time, in Kingston, the Jamaican entry to the annual Miss World contest is crowned at a gala pageant.

A charity event of special note is the Henry Morgan Buccaneer Ball in early October, held in the famous privateer's erstwhile headquarters of Port Royal, near Kingston. Guests don pirate garb—what else? About a week thereafter it's time for one of the oldest and most prestigious sportfishing contests in the Caribbean, the Port Antonio International Marlin Tournament.

The year rounds out with two of Jamaica's great loves, the show horse and golf. At the beginning of November, in Annotto Bay, the Jamaica Horse Association holds its annual International Horse Trials, two days of dressage, show jumping, and cross-country featuring teams from the U.S., Great Britain, and the host country. Around the third week of November, the Jamaica Open Golf Tournament draws to Kingston professionals and amateurs from around the world. Then, in mid-December, two dozen top golfers from the LPGA swing it out; and in mid-January, the Jamaica Classic draws international heavy hitters with a U.S. $500,000 purse. The place: Tryall Golf and Beach Club, Montego Bay.

INFORMATION, PLEASE

The single best source of information and assistance on the island is the Jamaica Tourist Board. Don't hesitate to contact one of the JTB offices before or during your stay. They're very helpful, and they can supply you with free travel brochures and maps.

In the United States: 866 Second Avenue, 10th Floor, New York, NY 10017, 212–688–7650; 36 South Wabash Avenue, Suite 1210, Chicago, IL 60603, 312–346–1546; 300 West Wieuca Road NE, Suite 100A, Atlanta GA 30342, 404–250–9971; 8235 Douglas Avenue NE, Suite 1000, Lock Box 18, Dallas, TX, 75225, 214–361–8778; 3440 Wilshire Boulevard, Suite 1207, Los Angeles, CA 90010, 213–384–1123.

In Jamaica, the JTB is headquartered at 21 Dominica Drive, New Kingston, 929–9200 (mailing address: Tourism Centre Building, New Kingston, Box 360, Kingston 5, Jamaica, W.I.). There are regional offices in Montego Bay (at Cornwall Beach, 952–4425), Ocho Rios (in the Ocean Village Shopping Centre, 974–2582), Port Antonio (at City Centre Plaza, 993–3051), Mandeville (at 21 Ward Avenue, 962–1072), and Negril (at Plaza de Negril, 957–4243).

Tourist board information desks are also staffed at the Montego Bay and Kingston airports.

The best island newspaper is the *Daily Gleaner*, though the *Star* is more lively; both provide useful updates on shopping, dining, nightlife, and special events. An especially good locally published guidebook is Margaret Morris's *Tour Jamaica*, available at many hotels and other tourist venues.

EXTRA "IRIE"

In the local patois, *irie* means the best imaginable. And if you're looking for a Jamaica beyond the simply great, the "Platinum Plan" is offered by **Elegant Resorts of Jamaica.** Under this plan, guests check into one of six ultraluxury resorts for a week—Tryall Golf and Beach Club, Round Hill, or Half Moon Club in Montego Bay; Plantation Inn or the San Souci Hotel and Club in Ocho Rios; or Trident Villas and Hotel in Port Antonio. Then, for no additional charge, they may spend a few nights and dine at any of the other five, not to mention special treats guests may receive such as flowers and champagne in suites, massages, and lots of personal attention from each property manager. For information call 800–237–3237.

Why not rent your own villa, complete with housekeeper (who can usually double as a nanny), gardener, and cook? Jamaica offers villas that run the gamut from quaint and cozy to palatial; from in-town to secluded seaside spots with private tennis courts, swimming pools, and even isolated stretches of beach. Listings of villa representatives are available through the Jamaica Tourist Board. Easier yet, phone the **Jamaica Association of Villas and Apartments** (JAVA) at 800–221–8830 (in Miami, 305–667–0179); this organization lists nearly 350 rental properties ranging from $750 to more than $4,000 per week.

Finally, for information about and reservations for dozens of small and mid-size hostelries across the island, all of reputable quality and most modestly priced, contact Jamaica Reservations at 800–526–2422.

WHAT TO TAKE

Packing shouldn't be a chore, since basic resortwear—shorts, slacks, sport shirts—will serve as the mainstay of your wardrobe. But your destination in Jamaica makes a difference. In Negril, where women can go topless at most beaches and clothing is optional for both sexes at others, casual is the operative word year-round. Yet even in Negril —as throughout the island—short shorts and bathing suits are not considered proper attire for shopping or dining in town, and in the evenings most women switch to pants or skirts.

And even vegetating on the beach means bringing along some cover-ups—long-sleeved shirt, pants, hat or sun visor. Base tan or not, don't forget sunscreen. If taken light-ly, the Caribbean sun is *not* forgiving.

In the more conventional resorts of Montego Bay, Ocho Rios, and Port Antonio, men are required to wear a jacket (and tie, except in summer) at cocktails and dinner. For the same reason, women should pack at least one light-weight "dress-up" outfit. And in Kingston, the island's gov-ernmental and business center, you will feel out of place altogether in shorts. Most Jamaican men in the capital wear long-sleeved shirts and trousers; the women, modestly cut dresses.

Up in the cooler mountains a sweater or light jacket will certainly come in handy.

Take the absolute minimum. Airlines restrict the num-ber and weight of bags you may bring—Air Jamaica, for instance, limits coach passengers to two checked bags apiece weighing not more than 120 pounds combined, and one carry-on bag. Save room to bring home that hand-carved ironwood walking stick or handmade hammock. The shops are also full of wonderfully colorful beach- and casu-al-wear.

Don't forget sunglasses and an appropriate beach read —such as *The Book of Jamaica* by Russell Banks, an account of the author's gradual absorption into the Maroon culture and his immersion into a new life as Johnny of Jamaica. Film is expensive on the island, so if you pack a camera, bring all you'll need. This applies to cigarettes and drug-store items as well. It's worth hauling along a small first-aid kit, plus remedies for headache and upset stomach, just in case. If you're traveling with a small child, disposable diapers, for-mula, and baby food are easily found in the main tourist areas—though, again, at higher prices than back home.

GETTING THERE

By air, Jamaica lies only 3½ hours from New York, less than 90 minutes from Miami, and about five hours from either Dallas or Los Angeles. Year-round Air Jamaica, the national carrier, flies its regular aircraft to both Montego

Bay and Kingston from Atlanta, Baltimore, Los Angeles, Miami, New York, Philadelphia, Tampa, and Toronto.

Eastern flies from Atlanta to Montego Bay on weekends and from Miami to Montego Bay daily. American Airlines has nonstop service to Kingston and Montego Bay daily from New York and Miami. Continental Airlines has daily service from Newark, New Jersey, and weekend service from Houston. Air Canada flies to both Kingston and MoBay from Toronto, five times a week. BWIA offers service from San Juan, Puerto Rico, to Kingston and Montego Bay.

The most convenient airport for travelers headed to Port Antonio or Mandeville is Kingston's Norman Manley Airport; those destined for Montego Bay, Ocho Rios, or Negril should use the airport at Montego Bay. Sometimes the most convenient option of all is to connect at an international airport to Trans Jamaican Airlines intraisland flights linking Kingston, Mandeville, Montego Bay, Negril, Ocho Rios, and Port Antonio.

Check with the airline or your travel agent for the latest on fares and their requirements. And remember that before your return, the airline requires reconfirmation of your reservation at least 72 hours prior to departure. Should you forget, your seat might be resold.

You might also investigate a money-saving package that combines airfare with a hotel room and other extras such as rental car, entertainment, and dining discounts. It's not uncommon that the total cost of such a package—eight days at a good beachfront hotel, say, plus roundtrip airfare and more—can be had for what you would ordinarily pay for airfare alone.

Of course, Jamaica is also a popular stopover for cruise ships plying the Caribbean. Most of these leave from Miami, Tampa, or Port Everglades, and their ports of call include Montego Bay, Ocho Rios, Port Antonio, and Kingston.

WHEN YOU ARRIVE

Upon arrival, you face the island's immigration and customs officials. For U.S. and Canadian citizens a passport (it can be up to a year beyond its expiration date) is identification enough but is not required; in its place *two* of the following may be presented: residency card or certificate (for legal residents who are not U.S. or Canadian citizens), naturalization certificate or card, driver's license with photo, voter's registration card, or birth certificate. Married women using birth certificates should also bring a copy of their marriage licenses.

Customs allows personal items duty free (though on the flight you will be asked to declare everything on a customs form). Not allowed are rum, pets, raw meats, flowers, and firearms.

There are no vaccination or other health requirements for entry (unless you are arriving from a country where serious contagion exists), nor do you need to take any special medical precautions. Even the water is safe to drink.

WHEN YOU LEAVE FOR HOME

Again, remember to reconfirm your airline reservation at least 72 hours in advance of your flight. And be sure to save enough Jamaican currency to pay the departure tax of J$80 per person.

As you scout the airport for ways to spend other remaining island currency, keep the following in mind:

Jamaican Blue Mountain coffee. The price for this world-renowned brew—whole beans or ground—is virtually the same throughout the country, even in the Blue Mountains. Roughly, it will cost about half what it goes for in most gourmet shops or coffee stores in the United States (the exact price, naturally, fluctuates with the exchange rate and market supply). If you intend to buy several pounds—attractively packaged in individual burlap coffee bags and vacuum-sealed foil for freshness—you might as well wait to buy your coffee at the airport just before departing.

Jamaican hot sauces and exotic jellies and jams from tropical fruits are excellent gifts. These can be bought at either international airport.

Fresh Jamaican flowers. Airport shops have inexpensive preboxed assortments of such beautiful tropical flora as anthurium and poinciana. Tempting as they are, an agricultural inspector will examine them petal for petal at the U.S. point of entry, and then may, or may not, allow them in.

Duty-free goods. These can be purchased with credit card, traveler's check, Jamaican, U.S., or Canadian currency. And don't forget that although "duty free" can mean prices as much as half off those charged back home, U.S. Customs *will* levy duty charges if you return with more than the allowable limit of $400, including one liter of alcohol per adult. Duty-free liquor, cigarettes, and Jamaican cigars can only be purchased at the pier or airport.

MONEY

Money matters can get a bit confusing, since Jamaicans also call their legal tender the dollar. And while new regulations require that Jamaican currency must be used for all cash purchases (except at duty-free shops, as noted above), the Jamaicans themselves, especially in prime tourist areas, sometimes quote prices in U.S. dollars. The difference is substantial: The rate of exchange is fixed at J$6.50 to the U.S.$1, with another devaluation to J$7 expected soon. Banks give the full legal exchange rate. Exchange bureaus, hotels, boutiques, and so forth, which often have a service charge, are offering J$6.30 to U.S.$1.

Currency can be exchanged at airport bank counters, cruise-ship piers, commercial banks, and in nearly all hotels. The daily rate is the same everywhere on the island, so your hotel is almost always the quickest and best place to buy Jamaican dollars. Banks are open between 9 A.M. and 2 P.M., Monday through Thursday; Fridays they close at noon, then reopen from 2:30 to 5 P.M.

Make sure to get a receipt. Without one, you won't be able to reconvert Jamaican currency before going home. Only airport and cruise-pier bank counters are authorized to reconvert—and it is illegal to take Jamaican dollars into or out of the country.

Of course, major credit cards and traveler's checks are also widely accepted by hotels, restaurants, and shops.

Note: Unless specifically noted otherwise, all prices quoted in this book are in U.S. dollars and are subject to fluctuations in the exchange rate. Room rates quoted exclude tax and service charge and are given for the high season (from mid-April to mid-December, they drop about 40%).

GETTING AROUND

Unless you must have one, don't rent a car for your entire stay. They are very expensive—a compact car with air-conditioning for a week, for instance, runs upward of $630. Gasoline is equally pricey—about $1.75 an imperial gallon (one-fifth larger than the U.S. gallon). Although the highways are generally good, they're poorly marked, if at all; and you've got to make the adjustment to driving on the left (this was a British colony, remember?).

If you still want a car, do reserve it beforehand, either with a direct phone call and a deposit sent to Jamaica, or via a company's 800 number with a credit card. If at all possible, get a written confirmation or reference number on your reservation. Cars are all but impossible to rent once you're on the island, especially in peak season. The big chains have toll-free numbers, so making reservations is easy; ask for a written confirmation and bring it with you.

You won't need an international driver's license. A valid U.S. or Canadian license is sufficient. But unless you are paying by credit card, you will be asked for a cash deposit of several hundred dollars.

Among the dozen or more rental outfits on the island, try: Avis (800–331–1212), Dollar (800–421–6868), Hertz

(800–654–3131), National (800–328–4567), or Island (926–8012 in Kingston, 952–5771 in Montego Bay).

A much less expensive and more adventuresome means of personal transport is a moped or motor scooter. These can be rented from most major hotels, or at rental agencies. Stony Hill Castle Ltd. Bike Rentals, with locations in Negril (next to the police station, 957–4460) and Montego Bay (Holiday Inn Village Shopping Centre, 953–2292), charges about $28 a day for a scooter and $40 for either a trail bike or Honda CM200 motorcycle, plus a deposit. In Ocho Rios, contact Motor Trails, Carib Arcade on Main Street (974–5058), who have scooters at a daily rate of $27.

Most visitors, though, find it best to rely on taxis for short hauls. Easy to find at airports and most hotels, they can also be summoned by telephone or hailed at curbside.

Keep in mind: Not all taxis are metered, so come to an understanding on the fare ahead of time. For out-of-the-way destinations, ask the cabbie to return for you at a specified time. From midnight to 5 A.M., a 25 percent surcharge is added to the metered fare or posted rate. All licensed taxis display red PPV (Public Passenger Vehicle) plates; a recent addition is a plate marked "Tourism" with a number that indicates that the taxi and driver have passed additional inspections.

In Kingston and Montego Bay, buses are frequent and a cheap means of transport. Check with the Jamaican Tourist Board offices for routes, rates, and times. Minibuses also run on these routes, but they're often so crowded that passengers literally hang off the sides.

There's yet another alternative: Jamaica Railway runs its diesel trains daily between Kingston and Montego Bay, a remarkable, inexpensive, five-hour journey that's sure to be memorable if you're in the mood and have the time to spare. About $4 first class (weekends only), $2.60 coach. Phone 922–6620 in Kingston; 952–4842 in Montego Bay.

The quickest means of travel between major points on the island is by air. Trans Jamaican Airlines (923–6664 in Kingston; 957–4251 in Negril; 952–5401 in Montego Bay; 974–3254 in Ocho Rios; 993–2405 in Port Antonio) connects Kingston, Montego Bay, Negril, Ocho Rios, and Port Antonio. Book in advance through a travel agent, if possible. The Kingston-to-Montego Bay fare, for instance, is $44; from MoBay to Negril, it's closer to $50.

A final transportation tip: Try to arrange your airport transfer in advance through a travel agent or when making hotel reservations (if that service is provided). Taxi fares from Montego Bay's Sangster Airport to local hotels will run perhaps $12, but to Ocho Rios it can cost upwards of $70, and runs about that to Negril. From Norman Manley Airport in Kingston to Port Antonio, it's as much as $80.

GUIDED TOURS

The tour operators are several, the options many, but well regarded are Greenlight Tours (952–2650 in Montego Bay, 929–7204 in Kingston) and Jamaica Tours (952–1398 in Montego Bay).

Half-day excursions are usually priced at under $20; a full day about $25, not including lunch.

Sights well worth touring with a guide include the Great Houses—Devon House, Greenwood, and Rose Hall —and the plantations—Brimmer Hall and Prospect—as well as Kingston, Montego Bay, and Ocho Rios.

From Montego Bay, the Hilton High Day Tour (also known as the "Up, Up and Buffet") costs a steep $58, with pickup from any main MoBay hotel, but is certainly the most uplifting tour on the island. After an early morning ride to a former banana plantation near Negril and a Jamaican breakfast, a tethered hot-air-balloon ride ($20 extra if taken alone) carries you aloft, albeit briefly; there follows a tour of the plantation and the German village of Seaford Town, a sumptuous suckling-pig luncheon, rum drinks, and per-haps a hike or horseback ride. The same tour can be ar-ranged from Negril. Reserve through your hotel, or phone 952–3343.

Another popular all-day experience is the Governor's Coach Tour. A railway coach car that once was the private conveyance of Jamaica's governors, now replete with a bar and calypso band, travels 40 miles into the interior from Montego Bay, with stops at the Appleton Rum Distillery, the Ipswich Caves, a charming riverbank for a picnic lunch, and Catadupa (where you can buy fabric for a dress or sport shirt on the way up and pick up the finished product on the way back). Tuesday through Friday the train pulls out of the station at 9:30 A.M. and returns at 5 P.M. A ticket goes for about $42, including lunch and a rum drink. Book as early as possible with Jamaica Tours (952–1398).

Several times a week, the newest and most elaborate train to the Appleton rum estate chugs its way at 8:50 A.M. from MoBay (witha 4:30 P.M. return). This comfortable, air-conditioned train has guides, drinks, and lunch as well as musicians, on board. After a stop at Catadupa to select a made-to-order shirt or skirt for pickup on the return trip, there's a full stop at the Appleton Rum Distillery and the Ipswich Caves. For $50, the folks from the Appleton Estate Express (592–3692 or 592–6606) fetch guests from MoBay hotels and deliver them back to their doors.

MEET THE PEOPLE

For two decades now, the Meet the People program has successfully brought together visitors and Jamaicans with similar backgrounds and interests. The Meet the People volunteers include teachers, nurses, musicians, sportsmen, artists, journalists, businessmen, and others with enthusiasms ranging from painting to polo to poker. Together, you might watch a play, go to church, or simply visit with the friends and family of your host.

The idea is to provide an opportunity for a cultural exchange that goes beyond the usual tourist experience, and it works. You might even make a real friend. Best of all, it's free of charge. Simply contact the nearest Jamaica Tourist Board office.

OTHER TIPS

● **Drugs.** Chances are, you *will* be approached by street "hustlers" peddling the renowned island marijuana—called *ganja*—or cocaine. Just remember that these drugs are illegal. Getting arrested with them in your possession will almost certainly result in a heavy fine, possible jail sentence, or an immediate trip home.

● **Electric current.** In most hotels, it's 110 volts, 50 cycle—just like at home. A few offer both 110 and 220. Those with only 220 usually supply converters or adapters for hair dryers and electric shavers.

● **Postage.** Postcards to North America, via airmail, require postage of 45 cents, Jamaican; letters are 55 cents per half ounce.

● **Tipping.** Restaurants and hotels often add a service charge, and thus no tipping is necessary; but it's best to inquire. Otherwise, 10 to 15 percent is fine. At some all-inclusive resorts, no tipping is allowed.

● **Photographs.** Jamaicans do not like to be snapped without permission. Ask first, and you'll almost always get a yes; sometimes a small tip is requested.

● **Water.** It's filtered and purified and safe to drink anywhere.

TIPS FOR BRITISH TRAVELERS

● **Government Tourist Office.** Contact the Jamaican Tourist Office (111 Gloucester Place, London W1H3PH, tel. 01–224–0505) for brochures and tourist information.

● **Passports and Visas.** You will need a valid, 10-year passport (cost: £15), and a valid return ticket. British citizens are not required to have visas. A yellow fever vaccination is required if you are entering Jamaica from an infected area.

● **Customs.** Jamaica has no restrictions on tobacco, alcohol, or luxury goods. You are not allowed to bring flowers, plants, honey, fruits, meats, or vegetables into the country.

Returning to the UK, you may take home, if you are 17 or over: (1) 200 cigarettes or 100 cigarillos or 50 cigars or 250 grams of tobacco; (2) two liters of table wine and (a) one liter of alcohol over 22% by volume (most spirits) or (b) two liters of alcohol under 22% by volume (fortified or sparkling wine); (3) 60 milliliters of perfume and ¼ liter of toilet water; and (4) other goods up to a value of £32.

● **Insurance.** We recommend that to cover health and motoring mishaps, you insure yourself with Europ Assistance (252 High St., Croydon, Surrey CRO INF, tel. 081–680–1234). It is also wise to take out insurance to cover the loss of luggage (but check that such loss isn't already covered in any existing homeowner's policies you may have). Trip-cancellation insurance is another wise buy. The Association of British Insurers (Aldermary House, Queen St., London EC4N 1TT, tel. 071–248–4477) will give comprehensive advice on all aspects of vacation insurance.

● **Tour Operators.** Here is a selection of the companies offering packages to Jamaica. Also contact your travel agent for the latest information:

Airtours PLC (Wavell House, Holcombe Road, Helmshore, Rossendale, Lancashire BB4 4NB, tel. 0706–260000) offers 14-night packages ranging from £399 to £600, and special *prestige* deals for up to £900. Of the less expensive packages there are self-catering holidays in shared apartments as well as bed-and-breakfast deals.

Kuoni Travel Limited (Kuoni House, Dorking, Surrey, RH5 4AZ, tel. 03–06–776711) offers seven-day deals at a range of hotels, costing from £488 to £1,675. In addition, Kuoni offers special "Two for One" and "Three for Two" packages to Jamaica, where, between April and December, one can get up to one week or two weeks free after staying one week.

Thomas Cook (Box 36, Thorpe Wood, Peterborough, Cambridgeshire PE3 6SB, tel. 0733–330300) offers packages for seven nights from £915 to £1,525. For 14 nights, the price ranges from £1,397 in the off-season to £2,320 at peak times.

Thomson Holidays (Greater London House, Hampstead Road, London NW1 7SD, tel. 071–387–1900) arranges seven-night stays in a variety of Jamaican hotels with prices ranging from £398 to £1,046. For a 14-night stay, the price ranges from £504 to £1,546.

Virgin Holidays (3rd Floor, Sussex House, High Street, Crawley, West Sussex RH101BZ, tel. 0293–775511) offers accommodations packages for seven nights ranging from £679 to £839, and from £889 to £1,139 for 14 nights.

● **Airfares.** *British Airways* is the only airline that flies direct to Jamaica from England. *Virgin Atlantic* has indirect service, with a stopover permitted in New York or Miami. APEX fares start at £462 in low season and £554 in high season.

The North Coast

This is the Jamaica of legend: the island paradise of sugar-soft sand and romantic waterfalls, the Blue Lagoon and reggae till dawn. This is the Jamaica that welcomes the winter-weary and the stressed-out and dedicates itself to rejuvenation and the perfect tan.

No two Jamaican beaches are the same. The resorts of the North Coast are as distinct in mood and style as are, say, New York and Los Angeles. Here's where to find *your* place in the sun for the perfect vacation you've always dreamed of.

A reminder: Hotel rates are in U.S. currency before tax and service charge; they are subject to fluctuations in the rate of exchange. We quote peak season figures. Prices from mid-April to mid-December drop about 40% so if your budget is a consideration you might think about visiting Jamaica during these off-peak months. Don't forget to send to any Jamaica Tourist Board office for the free listing of all hotel and guest-house rates (winter or spring/summer), which lists all the alternatives.

NEGRIL

Everything you've heard about Negril is true. Nestled at the island's westernmost point, it is the do-as-you-please capital of Jamaica. Casual to a fault, it is a barefoot paradise dedicated to whatever floats your boat. A few years back the pleasures of Negril were an open secret to wool-hatted Rastafarians, hedonistic wanderers, adventurous college kids, and those who wanted to sample the island's legendary *ganja* and other illicit substances with the least chance of rude interruption. Clothing was optional on its beaches, and life was sweet, *mon*.

Today, late-model hippies and swinging singles are being joined by an ever-growing number of peace-loving souls of every stripe who are attracted by Negril's justly renowned luminous white sand, lush greenery, and spectacular sunsets. Here, all manner of people, native and tourist, famous and infamous, wealthy and budget-minded, mingle with ease and affability.

LODGING

Accommodations in Negril reflect the diversity of its visitors, but all share one welcome characteristic: A strict code limits the height of buildings to that of the average palm tree. Thus, while you will find no high rises, your choices can span the gamut from all-inclusive splendor to a thatched-roof cottage.

About four miles north of the village, on the beach at Rutland Point, is the Club Med-like **Hedonism II** (957–4200), Box 25, Negril. Like several other havens of hedonism on the island, there are only two ground rules here: First, your room rate covers everything except phone calls and personal laundry—including the hotel's host of activities, meals, drinks, cigarettes, even tips. Next, if you don't arrive with a roommate, one (of the same sex) will be assigned to your room; and no one under 16 years of age may stay here.

What's to do here? How about lessons in horseback riding, sailing, parasailing, water-skiing, scuba, snorkel, and Jamaican culture? You'll also find six lighted tennis courts, swimming pool with whirlpool, Nautilus equipment, a library, and virtually nonstop fun-and-games activities like bikini-judging contests for both men and women. There are also two nude beaches, including one on Booby Cay (an awkward bird, by the way). When the sun goes down, you've already found one of the best discos on the entire island.

The 280 guests rooms in several two-story buildings are bright, modern, and recently refurbished; they are air-conditioned and have private baths. All this, for about $1,160 a week per person.

Just south along this strand of gorgeous beach, nearly hidden in the coconut palms, lies **Sandals Negril** (957–4216; toll-free 800–SAN–DALS), Box 12, Negril. More intimate than its rollicking neighbor, this resort is no less comprehensive. Stretched out along Negril's famed Seven Mile Beach, rooms here include junior suites and one-bedroom suites, all with secluded balcony and sea view. All water sports are included in the all-inclusive price. In addition, there's complimentary tennis, meals, drinks, and much more at this gem with 190 guest rooms. The weekly package runs in the vicinity of $2,260 to $3,050 per couple.

Super Clubs' **Grand Lido** (957–4010 or 800–858–8009), Box 88, Negril, offers a custom-designed all-inclusive vacation for the visitor willing to spend, who also expects a lot in return. This flagship of SuperClubs has 200 lushly appointed, oceanfront rooms with private patio, color television, direct dial phone, AM/FM cassette system. The entrance hall is a palatial expanse of marble, floors and columns, with a massive waterwheel turning as a working sculpture. Every conceivable sport, from scuba to tennis to fitness corners, is featured. Possibly best of all, there are sunset cruises on the 147-foot yacht *Zein*, once owned by Prince Rainier and Princess Grace. Now, Captain Wynne Jones of Wales presides over late-day sailings, private sea-going parties, and even weddings at sea. Weekly all-inclusive rates are roughly $1,610 per person and $3,220 per couple

A bit farther south along Norman Manley Boulevard, also known as Route A1—the road that traces the Seven

Mile Beach—is the **Negril Gardens** (957–4408; toll-free 800–243–9420), Negril P.O., Negril. In 1986, managing director John Sinclair opened his pink-and-white hostelry that includes a 2½ acre beach, including a charming open-air bar and restaurant and another bar and terrace overlooking a spacious pool and tennis courts.

All 56 rooms have colonial-style porches—where breakfast can be taken—and are air-conditioned, with pitched wood ceilings, carpeting, French windows, king or double beds, and satellite TV. The staff is helpful and efficient. The double-occupancy rate is $130 per night.

The **Negril Inn** (957–4209), Negril, Westmoreland, is an all-inclusive 46-room resort that offers some of the prettiest palm-speckled sandy beaches in Jamaica. The beach, in fact, is the center of virtually everything the Negril Inn offers guests. A pleasant restaurant, dancing, and entertainment are also featured. Expect to pay $130 per person, double occupancy.

A few minutes' drive from the roundabout that marks "downtown" Negril—and easy to miss from the highway—is the cozy and serene **Charela Inn** (957–4277), Box 33, Negril. The Spanish-style inn, housing a dining room that serves affordable Jamaican and French cuisine and a small bar, is steps away from the talc-smooth sand and the sea, or a fresh-water swimming pool. The Grizzles, who oversee this comfortable destination, know just about everything there is to know about Negril, and they can set you up in anything from a Sunfish to a yacht.

The best rooms are the pair over the dining room and the honeymoon suite up the spiral staircase; the others—there are only 36 in all—string away from the beach and do not have sea views. They are air-conditioned and have private baths. Rates start at $150 per night for two (plus $30 for the MAP plan).

New for the '90s is a resort for couples that promises "there are no limbo contests here." This is the 130 suite-only *Swept Away* (957–4040, Long Bay, Negril. Here, you'll find four two-bedroom villas, 16 four-bedroom atrium suites, and 58 one-bedroom garden suites, all fronted by a half mile of beach, rambling along 20 acres of lushly landscaped property. This comprehensive fitness facility features racquetball, squash and lighted tennis courts (hard surface or clay), exercise lap pool, fully equipped gym, aerobics, yoga, massage, steam, sauna, whirlpool, billiards, bicycles, seaside pool, Sunfish sailing, windsurfing, water-skiing, reef snorkeling, and scuba diving. Some accommodations even come with a private butler. All feature creative cuisine, from poolside juices and veggie bar, to gourmet pizzas, fresh pastas, and lots of fish or white meat. Weekly prices per couple range from $2,500 to $3,000.

EXPLORING

Those who seek out Negril solely to eat, drink, and be slothful are blessed. This is an ideal setting in which to perfect the art of all three, and there's little reason to do anything else. You'll risk no guilt trip by skipping the local museums and architectural marvels, because there are no local museums or architectural marvels.

The historically minded might note that the resort Hedonism II faces what is now called Negril harbor, but is better known as **Bloody Bay**—so named because whalers used to clean their catch here. It was also here that "Calico Jack" Rackham and his female partners in piracy, Anne Bonney and Mary Read, were caught in 1720.

Those who feel the need for excursion should consider these alternatives: Montego Bay is 47 miles distant along the coast-hugging Route A1. To the southeast, Savanna-la-Mar ("the plain by the sea"), a sugar port founded in 1703, is only 19 miles away. Its still-bustling wharf is near the end of Great George Street, the longest city street on the island, and next to the stone remains of the Old Fort (converted into a public swimming pool).

From here, by all means push on another 32 miles to **Black River,** with its many Georgian-style buildings; less than half-way there, on the grounds of Bluefields House near the Bluefields police station, is a breadfruit tree said by some to have been planted by the famous Captain Bligh in the 1790s.

Ten miles beyond Black River Route A2 brings you to Bamboo Avenue, a three-mile stretch of road between Holland Estate and Lacovia that is one of the most-photographed spots in Jamaica. Bamboos planted in the 19th century arch across the road from both sides, forming a living cathedral ceiling. Nearing this memorable sight, you pass through the Great Morass, a freshwater swamp that is also a crocodile refuge. Off Bamboo Avenue (near Middle Quarters), female vendors entice you with packages of plump, pink shrimp; they're delicious but not for the meek —they're peppery.

A more demanding trip takes you inland to Seaford Town, where many residents are descendants of early 19th-century German settlers, and to the edge of the mysterious Cockpit Country, much of which is still unexplored. The best course is to follow Route A2 past Savanna-la-Mar to Ferris Cross, then head north on Route B8 to the town of Whithorn; there, take the road that heads east through Darliston, Woodstock, Struie, and Rat Trap into Seaford Town. Figure two hours' driving time each way, at least, much of it on road surfaces of dubious quality.

There's an easier way to make this last excursion—and in addition to round-trip transportation it also includes breakfast, a tethered hot-air balloon ride, tour of a former banana plantation and Seaford Town, and a roasted suckling-pig luncheon. It's called "Up, Up and Buffet," costs about $55 per person ($20 extra for balloon ride), and leaves at 7 A.M. from Montego Bay daily except Monday and Saturday. Contact Hilton High, the tour operator, in Montego Bay (952–3343).

MONTEGO BAY

MoBay. Christopher Columbus called it "the gulf of good weather." It was once a prime exporter of sugar and bananas. Today it thrives because it is Jamaica's primary port for a major import—you, the visitor. Jamaica's second-largest city (population 43,500), Montego Bay exists almost wholly to serve the annual invasion of vacationers.

Jets stream in from cold northern cities, giving visitors an awe-inspiring aerial view of a gently undulating landscape dotted with velvety golf courses, swimming pools of all shapes and sizes, and winding streets, surrounded by a calm, clear sea that is a patchwork of blues and greens. Cruise ships glide past Doctor's Cave Beach, one of the island's best, and the bustle of the bay. No matter how you arrive, you'll find a place that can be both calming and confusing. But the more you know of its special places, the more you'll be seduced by MoBay and its multitude of charms.

LODGING

Nowhere else in the Caribbean is there a greater choice in type and style of accommodations. Head east from Donald Sangster International Airport (take Route A1, the Queen's Drive, until it intersects Kent Avenue, turn left), and you are only minutes away from **Sandals** (952–5510; toll-free 800–SAN–DALS), Box 100, Montego Bay. And at this all-inclusive beach resort, stretched out along the largest white-sand beach in Montego Bay, you and your significant other (Sandals "fits pairs") can partake of all or none of the host of activities. Food and drink, scuba and other water sports and lessons, constant games and contests, theme parties, plus use of the tennis courts, squash court, health club, pool, sauna, and Jacuzzi—it's all included in one package price for seven-night stays (three-nighters are available in off-peak months).

Package rates for the 243 air-conditioned rooms start at about $2,240 a week per couple and go as high as $2,950 a week for one-bedroom, beachfront villa suites.

Four miles east of the airport on Route A1, in an attractive arc around lush gardens and overlooking Mahoe Bay, is the **Sandals Royal Caribbean** (953–2231; 800–SAN–DALS), Box 167, Montego Bay. For couples only, this all-inclusive resort offers a private beach and a pool, three tennis courts (two are lighted), and a putting green. There are definite accents of elegance: breakfast brought to your door, fresh flowers placed in rooms. A dozen Jamaican colonial buildings contain 190 comfortable guest rooms with weekly rates, all meals and drinks included, from $2,240 to $2,800 per couple.

More traditional accommodations can be had a few miles further east, at **Holiday Inn Rose Hall** (953–2485; toll-free 800–465–4329), Box 480, Montego Bay. Its on-the-beach site, plus the recent complete overhaul of this high-rise by the Holiday Inn chain, make it a good choice for those who seek a familiar middle-of-the-road hostelry. The usual water-sports activities, a pool and private beach, decent food at the hotel restaurant, an arcade of shops, and popular nighttime entertainment are available. Its 516 rooms are air-conditioned and start at around $130 for a double.

Next to the Holiday Inn but truly a world apart is the **Half Moon Club** (953–2211), Box 80, Montego Bay. It is vast—some 400 acres, with the feel of an exclusive country club. It is deluxe—some villa suites have private pools. And since 1955 it has provided about as much luxury and as many top-shelf diversions as any resort in the Caribbean. The spectacular 18-hole Robert Trent Jones golf course has a club house that becomes a fine dining room in the evenings. On the mile-long private beach, a full spectrum of water sports is available; or you may stick with one of the seldom-busy freshwater pools. There are four night-lighted squash courts, 13 tennis courts (pro on duty, seven lighted), and a health spa; horseback riding can be arranged.

The Sunday buffet lunch is special, as are bonfire barbecues on the beach.

Managing Director Heinz Simonitsch has presided over this property from the beginning and oversees all renovations (most done by noted architect Earl Levy, owner of Trident Villas). This team has combined taste and elegance, both evident in the 208 spacious rooms, suites, and private villas that dot the landscape, at a winter MAP price of $340, double. Also, for those who favor the all-inclusive approach, the four-day, three-night "Platinum Plan" provides a room plus all meals, drinks, sports, and airport transfers for $1,400 to $2,570 per couple.

Following completion of an $11-million refurbishment program, the **Wyndham Rose Hall Beach and Country Club** (953–2650; toll-free 800–822–4200), Box 999, Montego Bay, reopened its doors and manicured grounds with meeting groups and conventions in mind. About nine miles east of the airport, this is another island property that has been upgraded and is now managed by the Dallas-based hotel chain. The beachfront location, as you would expect, means that all manner of water sports are only steps from your room; there's also a good-sized pool, an 18-hole championship golf course, and a half-dozen tennis courts with a pro for lessons. Dining possibilities include the Great House Verandah, in the main high-rise hotel, or the country club; the Junkanoo disco for late-night dancing. Recovery can be scheduled the following morning in the new Health Club.

In all, 500 well-appointed, air-conditioned rooms, each with private balcony, are housed in twin seven-story towers. They range from $150 to $205, double. (No MAP plan available at present.)

Other lodging choices await farther downtown. (From the airport, take Route A1, the Queen's Drive, until it forks into Sunset Avenue, which ends at Kent Avenue, the hotel action strip along the waterfront.) The **Toby Inn** (952–4370), 1 Kent Avenue, Montego Bay, is perfect for the budget-minded. This intimate, casual, in-town hostelry set amid gardens has a pool, a Chinese-Polynesian restaurant, and a coffee shop. Both Cornwall and Doctor's Cave beaches are a short walk away. Many places to eat, shop, and play are within easy hiking distance. All rooms have private bath; some are air-conditioned, some have paddle fans. They go for as little as $75 a night for a double.

The **Carlyle on the Bay** (952–4140; reservations at 800–SAN–DALS), Box 412, Montego Bay, is on the inland side of the road, but there's nearby beach access and a pool on the premises. This is a cheery, friendly place with a much-frequented pub and dining room; often there is entertainment in the evening. Fifty-two balconied rooms afford sea views; all have air-conditioning and private bath. This is a warm, casually elegant addition to the Sandals roster, with an accent on personal service, that draws a heavy repeat list of international guests. Weekly packages cost $1,450 to $1,560 per couple.

Fantasy Resort (952–4150), 2 Kent Avenue, Montego Bay, is a nine-story affair with a Mediterranean flavor. It's on the inland side of the road, but Doctor's Cave Beach is an easy jaunt. Its impressive saltwater pool is usually busy. There's a dining room, open-air bar, shopping arcade, and disco as well. The 119 air-conditioned rooms have private baths and terraces. Following a refurbishment at the start of the 1990s, double rates run about $100 a couple, E.P.

Next door is the moderately priced **Doctor's Cave Beach Hotel** (952–4355), Box 94, Montego Bay. Although not on the beach, this is a comfortable and convenient place, and the glorious sand is a short walk away. There is a pool, pleasant terrrace restaurant, and frequent entertainment. These 90 air-conditioned rooms, all with private bath, go for about $100 to $160 double.

Perched 500 feet above sea level, on a quiet hillside above town, the **Richmond Hill Inn** (952–3859), Box 362, Montego Bay, is an 18th-century great house that affords an exemplary view of MoBay itself as well as of the surrounding tropical coastline. The hotel is justly famed for its romantic terrace restaurant, which serves some of the best Jamaican cuisine in the area, and its busy bar. The beach is a few minutes' car or taxi ride away, but there's a pool. The 20 guest rooms are modern, air-conditioned, and have private baths. A double room costs about $115 a night, E.P.

Ten miles west of town along the coastal Route A1, on a lush and green peninsula, is a classically elegant enclave that enjoys an international reputation. **Round Hill** (952–5150), Box 64, Montego Bay, is set on 98 garden acres. Most of the accommodations here are privately owned villas, several with private pools, all with loyal staff, available for rent in the owners' absence. There's an exquisite private beach where every variety of water sport is pursued by day, lavish barbecues by night. Tennis can be enjoyed on the grounds; golf privileges are extended at nearby Tryall Golf and Beach Club.

Dinner and dancing (jacket and tie or black tie on Saturdays) in the rambling Pineapple House, the main building, is often followed by a nightcap in the bar huddled around the same piano played by Noel Coward, Cole Porter, Irving Berlin, and Leonard Bernstein. It is considered by many in the international set to be the finest accommodation in the Caribbean.

The 110 units include 36 guest rooms in Pineapple House (available in winter only). Villa suites range from about $330 to $470 a night, breakfast and dinner included;

the hotel rooms, closer to the sea, are $280, also with two meals a day.

A dozen miles west of town lies another oasis, the *Tryall Golf, Tennis and Beach Club* (952–5110; toll—free 800–336–4571), Sandy Bay Post Office, Hanover, Montego Bay. Historic and scenic, the Tryall Great House, built on a hilltop in 1834, is reminiscent of the days of the original planters, with a pristine white exterior and English chintz featured in the interior. Now, as the resort name indicates, both tennis and golf are the games here.The 18-hole course is the best on the island, and annually plays host to the LPGA; it's also one of the most beautiful, with stunning seaside views. And the beach part? It's a lovely crescent—recently improved—where water sports can be enjoyed with abandon. The Beach Cafe in the clubhouse is perfect for a casual water's edge lunch, and the great house has a dining room noted for its international cuisine and evening entertainment on the terrace. And there's a swim-up bar at the main pool.

Main pool? Yes, secluded among the trees and gardens of Tryall's rolling 2,200 acres are 40 villas, each with its own swimming hole, cook, chambermaid, laundress, and gardener. As at Round Hill, the villas are privately owned but can be rented. Two bedrooms go for $3,750 per week, three bedrooms for $5,000, and four bedrooms for $6,000. In the great house, another 52 distinctive guest rooms range from $340 to $410 per night, including breakfast and dinner.

Exploring

Echoes of Montego Bay's past are faint, but resonant. Shortly before Queen's Drive ends at the roundabout, a trio of cannons pointing seaward signal the remains of 16th-century **Fort Montego.** Continuing south onto St. James Street, the main drag through town, brings you to **Sam Sharpe Square** (formerly Charles Square and The Parade). The intriguing little structure in the square's northwest corner is The Cage.

The Cage was erected in 1806 as a jail for slaves and runaway seamen, and today it houses a small museum of

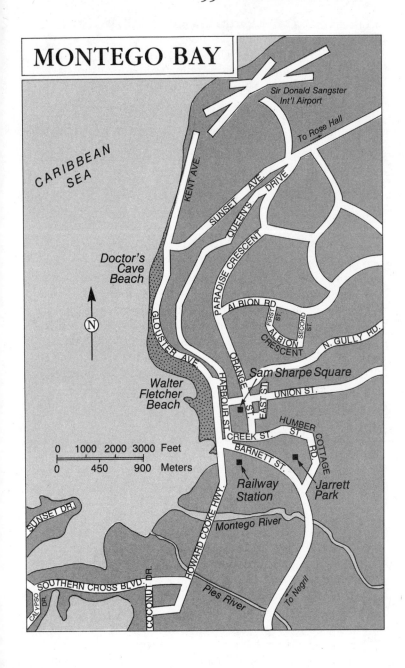

MONTEGO BAY

CARIBBEAN SEA

Sir Donald Sangster Int'l Airport

To Rose Hall

KENT AVE.

SUNSET AVE.

QUEEN'S DRIVE

PARADISE CRESCENT

Doctor's Cave Beach

N

ALBION RD.

FIRST ST.

SECOND ST.

N. GULLY RD.

ALBION CRESCENT

GLOUSTER AVE.

ORANGE ST.

Sam Sharpe Square

Walter Fletcher Beach

HARBOUR ST.

EAST ST.

UNION ST.

HUMBER ST.

COTTAGE RD.

CREEK ST.

BARNETT ST.

0   1000 2000 3000 Feet
0   450   900 Meters

Railway Station

Jarrett Park

SUNSET DR.

HOWARD COOKE HWY.

Montego River

SOUTHERN CROSS BLVD.

CALYPSO DR.

COCONUT DR.

Pies River

To Negril

pre- and postslave era artifacts and artwork. It's open 10 A.M. to 6 P.M. daily.

A few blocks east, at Union and East streets, a crumbling stone amphitheater is another remnant of the slave trade. Known as **The Slave Ring,** it is said to have been the town slave market.

Southeast of the square, at Church and St. Claver streets, limestone **St. James Parish Church** is set in a lovely tropical garden and is itself an admirable restoration (after a 1957 earthquake) of a handsome 1775 Georgian structure. Check out the elegant monuments inside.

West of the square lies Harbour Street, abustle with fishermen unloading their catch and burly stevedores handling fruit, produce, and other local goods for shipment. The **Crafts Market** is here also. To experience a market the way Jamaicans themselves do, try the **Public Market** (officially the Fustic Street Market, but only cartographers use that name). Continue south from the square to Barnett Street; Fustic intersects less than a half mile further, on the right. Especially on a Friday or Saturday, the place is a carnival of sights, sounds, and smells. Come prepared to bargain with the women higglers who run the show.

If you venture nowhere else beyond the party atmosphere of Montego Bay, consider the day-long Governor's Coach tour, also known as the Catadupa Choo Choo. You ride from MoBay some 40 miles into the mountainous interior in a railroad coach that used to be the private saloon car of Jamaican governors, replete with a calypso band and bar. Stops include the Appleton Rum works at Maggotty, the Ipswich Caves, and the Cockpit Country village of Catadupa, where local seamstresses will fit you for a shirt or dress, then deliver the finished product on your way back. This special excursion is run by Jamaica Tours (952–2887) and departs at 9:30 A.M. from Montego Bay railroad station Tuesday through Friday. A ticket is about $35 per person, including lunch and rum punch. Make reservations early.

A newer, air-conditioned train, the *Appleton Estate Express* (592–3692 or 592–6606), covers basically the same route for $50 per person, with extras added (see Guided Tours under General Information, above).

Another satisfying rail trip is aboard a diesel running daily between MoBay and the capital city of Kingston. The

four-and-a-half-hour trip costs only about $5 for first class
(weekends only), $3 coach, one way. See a lot of interesting
country in half the time (at roughly half the fare) by getting
off at the town of Williamsfield; a 15-minute bus or taxi ride
takes you to the town of Mandeville. If you'd rather let
someone else handle the arrangements, Premier Tours
(952–5919) hosts a Thursday 7 A.M. pickup at your hotel
and train ride to the Appleton Rum works, with a bus tour
of Mandeville. A fare of about $45 includes breakfast, sev-
en-course lunch at the Hotel Astra in Mandeville, rum
punch, and entertainment en route.

Rather travel by water? At the Martha Brae River in
Falmouth, 23 miles east of Montego Bay on Route A1, you
can hire a bamboo raft for two, poled by an experienced
raftsman. Start upriver at the Rafter's Village (follow the
signs off the coast highway), which has a restaurant, bar, and
shops. The leisurely trip toward the sea takes an hour and
a half and costs about $26 per person (afterwards, you'll be
driven back to your starting point). If you wish, make all the
arrangements, including transportation from MoBay and
back, at your hotel tour desk.

"Up, Up and Buffet" is a day tour that begins with
pickup at your hotel, a trip to a former banana plantation
and breakfast, a tethered balloon ride, roast suckling pig
lunch, tour of the village of Seaford Town, a German settlement, and more. The whole package costs about $55 per
person ($20 extra with the balloon ride). Contact Hilton
High (952–3343), Box 313, Montego Bay.

Would-be Indiana Joneses may wish to brave the un-
tamed Cockpit Country. It's here that the descendants of
the fierce Maroons—former slaves of the Spanish—and
other "free coloureds" fought such a successful guerrilla
war against the British that they won self-rule in a 1735
treaty that continues to this day. The "Land of Look Behind," where British colonials rode back-to-back on a single
horse to avoid ambush, begins only some 15 miles from
Montego Bay, at Maroon Town. Maroons no longer live
here but are concentrated around their capital of Accom-
pong, further into the rugged interior. It's recommended
that before venturing into this primitive enclave, you contact the Jamaica Tourist Board office in MoBay for information about minibus tours and guides.

For a much more tranquil experience, head off to Lisa Salmon's bird sanctuary, the **Rocklands Feeding Station** (952–2009) in the village of Anchovy. Take Route A1 west to Route B8 south; it's about four miles in all. Miss Salmon, a painter and naturalist, settled here in the 1950s and has since offered safe haven to some 140 species, many of which alight daily to be fed from 3:15 until 5 P.M. You are welcome to watch, quietly. Admission is $4, and no children under five years of age are allowed. By prearrangement with Miss Salmon, active bird-watchers may arrive at 7 A.M. with binoculars and a tape recorder.

If you'd like a peek at the way Jamaica's rich lived two centuries ago, you need not travel far. The most famous— or infamous—of these restored mansions is **Rose Hall** (953–2323). Built around 1770 as the showplace of the Caribbean, its reputation is due in equal measure to the ghost said to haunt its elegant, antique-filled rooms. A few years back, thousands of onlookers watched as psychics tried to make contact with Annie Palmer, the second mistress of Rose Hall, who supposedly did in three husbands, as well as a plantation overseer and any number of slaves who were her lovers; she herself was murdered in her bed in 1833. (If this sounds the stuff of fiction, find a copy of Jamaican novelist Herbert deLisser's *The White Witch of Rose Hall.*)

The furnishings at Rose Hall, though many are of museum quality, are not original. A small restaurant, Annie's Pub and bar have been added (near the torture chamber). In short, this is the most show-bizzy of the great houses in the area, but still definitely worth a look-see. It commands a ridge just beyond the Half Moon resort on Route A1, seven miles east of Montego Bay. Open every day from 9 A.M. to 6 P.M. Admission is $8.50 for adults, $4 for children.

Recently started are two new ways of visiting Rose Hall. On Wednesday nights, 7–10, there are Spooky Candlelight Tours (953–2323) that really are spooky, complete with tea-leaf readings by an English expert. Add nonstop "witches brew," Jamaican dishes, and hot reggae or calypso music, and you have a good way to spend an evening for $35, with pickup and return to MoBay hotels.

In a change of mood are Sunday afternoon (3–5) teas (953–2323), also with pickup and return to MoBay hotels, for $30 per person. These teas include tour of the mansion, opera recital, and a fashion show of Jamaican designs.

If you have time, look for the side road at the edge of Rose Hall. A walled cemetery a few hundred yards down is the family plot for relatives of poet Elizabeth Barrett Browning, whose father was born at Cinnamon Hill Great House farther along this road. Not open to the public, this restored mansion is owned today by country-and-western singer Johnny Cash. A bit further, ask a local "guide" to show you the waterfall used in the James Bond movie *Live and Let Die.*

Back on Route A1, about 15 miles east of MoBay, is **Greenwood** (information via the Trelawny Beach Hotel, 954–2450), another great house built by the Barretts, who once owned all the land from Rose Hall to Falmouth. Now owned by Bob and Ann Betton, who will share the many legends that have grown up around the property, the house has Barrett family portraits and the family Wedgwood china, as well as a fine library with books dating from 1697 and a collection of rare music boxes and musical instruments. Greenwood is open daily from 9 A.M. to 6 P.M.; admission is about $6.

FALMOUTH

This is a picturesque sugar port of Georgian homes and broad streets. It makes for a pleasant excursion for visitors staying in either Montego Bay (23 miles east) or Ocho Rios (44 miles west), but is also a worthy island address in itself— especially for those wanting to stake out a quieter, less crowded claim on the north shore. And because of its central location, it's easy to explore the coastline in both directions.

LODGING

There's only one resort we recommend in Falmouth, but the **Trelawny Beach Hotel** (954–2450), Box 54, Falmouth, offers as much value as any on the island. Set amid pleasant gardens, this 350-room, seven-story hostelry has both private beachfront and a large pool. The lobby and other public areas are attractive and airy.

Activities abound, and most are free, including scuba (one free tank dive per day), snorkeling, Sunfish sailing, windsurfing, water-skiing, glass-bottom-boat rides, tennis and tennis instruction (on four Laykold courts), reggae dance and craft classes, and live entertainment nightly. There's also a daily free shuttle service to Montego Bay, cruises on the hotel's 40-foot sailboat, and a discount on food, drink, and fishing charters at Falmouth Yacht Club.

Guests choose between two meal plans—either all meals included, or just breakfast and dinner. If this is beginning to sound like another of Jamaica's popular all-inclusive hotels, that's *almost* right. Liquor is not included in the room rate, which makes this a favorite for families. In fact, there's a daily schedule of children's activities, with specially designated hotel personnel to supervise them; baby-sitters are also easily booked. In summer, children (14 years and under) stay and eat for free when accompanied by an adult. At the same time, honeymoon and wedding (the hotel arranges for a justice of the peace, marriage license, and witnesses) packages are also popular here. There is no age restriction or required minimum stay. All this adds up to what the Trelawny Beach calls the "inclusive resort for everyone."

All 350 rooms are air-conditioned and have a private balcony or patio. Double occupancy costs $110–$120 per person with meals. The hotel has 40 cottage units that are especially good for families. Finally, inquire about package deals that include airfare—these can make staying here amazingly inexpensive.

EXPLORING

Most of Falmouth was built in the late 1700s, and its fine Georgian architecture is shown off to best advantage on Market Street, just west of Water Square at the center of town. Note especially the **Methodist Manse,** a stone-and-wood house with wrought-iron balconies built in 1799. From the square you can admire one of the best Georgian buildings in Jamaica—it's now used by the town council.

It's in Martha Brae—named for an Arawak Indian girl gifted, it's said, with supernatural powers—that you can hire a bamboo raft and river guide for an hour's leisurely float toward the sea.

East on Route A1, shortly before the Trelawny Beach, is a speck on the map known as Rock. There's a phosphorescent lagoon here where tiny organisms in the water glisten at night when the water is disturbed; fishing charters also leave from here. Another eight miles east, at Duncans, a right onto Route B10 will take you to the **Long Pond Sugar Factory and Distillery** (954–2401), where Gold Label Rum is made; tours are available by appointment. Below Clark's Town, another right turn, at Kinloss, brings you to the outskirts of the Cockpit Country.

Back on A1, it's six more miles from Duncans to Rio Bueno (you can also reach it from Clark's Town by taking Route B11 east to B5 north), a quaint fishing village on a horseshoe-shaped harbor with a photogenic waterfront church, old stone houses, and the ruins of Fort Dundas, which was built in 1778. Some historians believe Christopher Columbus made his first landing on the island here in 1494.

Six miles farther is Discovery Bay, so named because it has long claimed to be the site of Columbus's first landing, though the revisionist school of thought holds that he dropped anchor here on his fourth and final voyage, in 1503. In any event, Columbus Park offers an open-air museum where cannons and relics from sugar mills are on display on a limestone cliff overlooking the bay. The business of the bay these days is bauxite. Should you wish, guided tours of the **Kaiser bauxite mine and plant** (973–2221) can be arranged by appointment.

RUNAWAY BAY

With the sun-dappled sea to your left, sugarcane fields, pasture lands, and mountain vistas to your right, the north-shore drive continues. Goats and chickens forage at the highway's edge, Jamaicans go about their everyday business, and every few miles the auto traffic slows as another town looms into view.

LODGING

The highlight here is the intriguing **Jamaica Jamaica** (973–2436), Box 58, Runaway Bay. As the name implies, here's the place to "do as the Jamaicans do," but on a grand scale. The music, the parties, the food—all have gone native. This, too, is an all-inclusive property and is limited to adults (over age 16). The freebies include romantic horse-and-buggy rides and a year-round "golf school," in addition to the nonstop roster of sports.

There's a waterfall, Jacuzzi, lap pool, and exercise room—and that's just in the lobby area, which also has a bar, shops, and more. Many of the guest rooms have been given outlandishly large bath tubs. What else is there to do? There's the beach-cum-bar, tennis, an 18-hole golf course at a nearby country club, and if that's not enough, shopping and sightseeing shuttles. Week-long stays are about $1,200 per person.

FDR (800–859–8009), Runaway Bay, is another concept of an all-inclusive started by Frank Rance, who's also part of the SuperClubs upper echelon. The initials are based on the principles of "Man Fridays" or "Girl Fridays," who wait outside your suite door to do your bidding, as well as make the bed, cook, and act as a personal valet. The aim here is to draw families at about $1,200 per person, per week, with a child staying free in his/her parents' room. There's a child center, computer center, tennis court, disco, piano bar, water sports, and unlimited golf at nearby Runaway Bay Golf course.

It's a shame more visitors don't know about **H.E.A.R.T. Country Club** (973–2671), Box 98, St. Ann, perched above Runaway Bay and brimming with the island's true character. The club trains young Jamaicans who are interested in the tourism industry and provides a remarkably quiet and pleasant stay for guests at $60 per night, double occupancy. It's also an excellent place to book a table for a very reasonable dinner, prepared and served by Jamaica tourism trainees.

EXPLORING

Some 10 miles east of Runaway Caves, look for signs near the intersections of Routes A1 and A3 to the little town of St. Ann's Bay. Black nationalist hero Marcus Garvey was born here in 1887, and his monument presides in front of the town library. Just east of town is **Drax Hall,** where England's Prince Charles has played polo and Jamaicans do likewise.

OCHO RIOS

Ocho Rios is an overgrown, fun-loving village fringed by a ribbon of white sand. It is both a great place to stay and a great place to stop—it is also the island's foremost cruise-ship destination. Translation: The streets are often crowded.

LODGING

About a five-minute drive west of Ocho Rios is another Sandals property, **Sandals Dunn's River** (972–1610; toll free 800–SAN–DALS), Mammee Bay, which opened in the summer of 1990. It seems the Sandals formula is guaranteed for success, with its all-inclusive price for all ammenities, always with couples in mind. The 258-room resort gleams with an Italian Renaissance feeling, from cream exterior towers to high-domed ceilings. The emphasis here is on specialty restaurants (West Indian, Italian, Japanese), an extensive fitness center, and trips to nearby Dunn's River Falls.

If it's the big, boisterous, no-surprises atmosphere of a mass-market hotel you seek, the **Mallards Beach** (974–2200), Box 245, Ocho Rios, is your kind of place. Especially, we'd add, if there's an attractive package deal available. The largest resort in town, it has everything you'd expect: beach, pool, tennis courts, volleyball, Ping-Pong, health club, shops, disco, two restaurants, bar, and coffee shop. It's also within walking distance of the Ocean Village Shopping Centre and neighboring beachfront hostelries.

The Mallards Beach's 375 rooms range from $140 to $160, double; one-bedroom suites go for about $260 a night.

Just up the beach you will find the **Club Americana** (974–2151), Box 100, Ocho Rios, the Mallards Beach's virtual twin in terms of style, approach, and amenities. Here, again, look for the right all-inclusive deal, then enjoy this 11-story tower's five restaurants (the Victoria is fanciest), two swimming pools, tennis courts, and ideal location. Its 325 air-conditioned rooms start at $115 to $150 double, per person, per day.

A world apart but actually just beyond Mallards Bay is the homey **Hibiscus Lodge** (974–2676), Main Street, Box 52, Ocho Rios. You're still within a short stroll of the center of town, restaurants, and shopping, but the mood is far removed from the big-name hotels and steamy couples resorts. This is a destination favored by savvy Europeans, and it's easy to see why. Golfers have the use of the Upton Country Club south of town. And even though the lodge itself is on the captivatingly blue water, it is more reminiscent of Capri than the Caribbean. A stone staircase leads down a 30-foot cliff to a spit of sand that is protected by a reef ideal for snorkeling. The kitchen of the lodge's extremely popular, open-air Almond Tree restaurant is presided over by a Swiss-born chef.

Here is the place to hide or seek, at your pleasure. The inn's 26 rooms are modern and comfortable, have private baths, and all overlook the sea. Best of all, they rent in the $60-per-night range, double.

About two miles east of the center of town, on the coastal Route A3, the **Plantation Inn** (974–2501), Box 2, Ocho Rios, sits on 10 splendid acres of tropical hillside and white-sand beach. Without question among the finest resorts in the Caribbean, this elegant retreat has been satisfying visitors with discriminating taste for more than three decades by providing uncommonly high standards of service and comfort. Breakfast is served in the privacy of your room balcony. Mid-afternoon tea is a daily ritual. And dinner is a gourmet affair followed by dancing on the starlit veranda.

The beach—actually twin crescents of sand—is a climb down flower-edged steps. Water sports are superb. For diving, there's a spectacular technicolor reef 100 yards offshore. There are also two tennis courts, a pool, shops, and complimentary greens fees at nearby Upton Golf and Country Club.

Impeccably furnished, the 77 guest rooms range from about $350 a night, while suites go for $420 to $950. Breakfasts and dinners are included.

Another grand old seat of hospitality shares Sandy Beach Bay. Just a short distance farther along the coast route is the polished brass plaque on a stone pillar announcing the entrance to the small, classic **Jamaica Inn** (974–2514; toll-free 800–243–9420), Box 1, Ocho Rios. Service and surroundings have built up a loyal clientele since the inn opened in 1951, and often it's difficult for a newcomer to find a vacancy although it's worth a try.

The inn is perched on a cliff above a private paradise

of beach, where Sunfish and snorkel gear are available for rental. A rum punch from a white-jacketed waiter is yours for the asking—compliments of the house—while you sun. Tennis is available on the premises, and riding and golf (at Upton Country Club) are quickly arranged. The Continental and local cuisine in the dining room is excellent.

Each of the 45 lovely rooms has a private veranda suitable either for splendid isolation or entertaining friends. The stay is worth it, even with rates that range from $320 to $375, double, with all meals included.

Another in the ever-growing roster of successful couples-only all-inclusives, **Sandals Ocho Rios** (974–5691; toll-free 800–SAN–DALS) opened on nine acres in late 1988. It follows the formula perfectly, with plenty to do and no mandate to do anything. There are 237 units in four grades, from deluxe ocean view to standard.

Pastel-pink and white buildings terrace down a lush hillside to private Little Bay at the **Sans Souci Hotel and Club** (974–2353; toll-free 800–237–3237), Box 103, Ocho Rios. About four miles east of the town center on Route A3, the Sans Souci, which is nothing short of a tropical oasis, is one of the most splendidly decorated resorts in the Caribbean.

Day begins with breakfast served on your private balcony, which is angled for a stunning sea view. Early morning yoga or stretching classes start your day, then perhaps it's off to the beachfront water-sports center for sailing, snorkeling, water-skiing, diving, or a fishing trip; or to the tennis club for one of the four Laykod courts (two night lighted). How about a round of golf at nearby Upton Country Club instead? Horseback riding, a class in dressage, or a polo game can all be found at nearby Chukka Cove, the finest equestrian center in the Caribbean. If you'd rather relax at poolside, take your pick. In addition to its freshwater pool, there's also a natural, spring-fed pool whose waters have a mineral content comparable to that at spas of Europe.

The mineral springs under the San Souci property have been well-known for their therapeutic effects since the 1700s, but it wasn't until the 1986 that the mineral pool area became a fully equipped spa. It was affectionately named Charlie's Spa for the giant green sea turtle that has lived in its personal mineral pool for at least 18 years. Seven-day spa programs are offered on a "his and her" individualized regimen, with personalized "Charlie's Menus" for spa participants.

For dining in style, the award-winning Casanova restaurant is arguably the best in Ocho Rios. For those who are do-it-yourselfers, the suites come with kitchenettes. All 80 stylish units are air-conditioned and also have ceiling fans. Rates go from $350 to $550 for two, breakfast and dinner included. The spa program of seven days and six nights costs $3,200 for two.

Couples (974–4271), Tower Isle, St. Mary, is some 20 minutes' drive east along the north shore past Ocho Rios. This is the place that began the Club Med–like, adults-only, all-inclusive craze on the island in 1978, and its popularity is evident in its occupancy rate—the highest of any resort in Jamaica. Little wonder. It seems the management has thought of everything—and *everything* is included in the weekly rate.

The list is long: all meals, including liquor and midnight snacks, cigarettes, talent shows, piano bar, all manner of water sports (including deep-sea fishing and scuba), Nautilus gym, tennis, pool, nude and non-nude beaches, volleyball, Ping-Pong, two squash courts, horseback riding, bicycling . . . there's more, but you get the idea.

All 152 cheerful rooms have private bath, airconditioning, a private balcony or patio. Figure on about $2,500 per couple for seven days, six nights in peak season. Remember, no children or solitary travelers are allowed.

EXPLORING

Dunn's River Falls (974–2857) and beach, a few miles west of Ocho Rios, is *the* must-see along this stretch of the north shore. And it is indeed one of Jamaica's chief natural wonders—a clear mountain stream that cascades in tiers for 600 feet to a pristine beach and the sea. The goal is to climb to the top, an arduous but exhilarating experience. You can do it on your own, joining in the human daisy chain that gingerly works its way up; or you can hire a guide who knows the slippery spots and will safeguard your camera and snap your photo as you climb.

A bathing suit is the proper uniform for this mini-adventure. There are changing facilities here, as well as snack bars and souvenir sellers. Stairs lead down a tunnel under Route A1 to the beach, where you can rent a locker for your valuables. Then you must buy a ticket—for about 50 cents, available daily during daylight hours—to make the climb.

A three-mile stretch of Route A3 south of town is known as Fern Gully, in which the road snakes down an old riverbed that is shaded by the lush, cool green of giant ferns. Watch for **Shaw Park Gardens** on a hilltop west of the roadway (the Ruins restaurant—a beautiful place to see or sip a drink, not so terrific to dine—is just below); there are 34 acres with gorgeous views of Ocho Rios below, pretty ponds and meandering streams, as well as many tagged varieties of trees and flowers. Perfect for a quiet stroll or picnic; admission $3 per person, daily from 8 A.M. to 5 P.M.; 974–2552.

Should you be in the mood for a longer excursion, the southern route (Route A3 to A1) through the interior—over Mount Diablo and through the awesome gorge of Bog Walk—leads to Spanish Town and the capital city of Kingston. The total distance is 58 miles, but plan on a driving time of one-and-a-half to two hours.

East of the center of Ocho Rios, near the White River, is a sign pointing to the route inland to **Prospect Estate** (974–2058), a working banana and cassava plantation that offers guided tours. Tours run Monday through Saturday, at 10:30 A.M., 2 P.M., and 3:30 P.M.; on Sunday, at 1:30 P.M. and 3 P.M. Admission is $7.50 per person.

A short way farther along the coast highway (Route A3) is **Harmony Hall** (974–4222), a restored 19th-century great house that contains a gallery displaying Jamaican arts and crafts, as well as a bar and restaurant. It's open every day from 10 A.M. to 6 P.M.

The newest "must" in Ocho Rios is **Carinosa Gardens** (974–5346), a pet project of former Prime Minister Edward Seaga. This 20-acre garden on a hillside displays some of the loveliest orchids anywhere, plus a dramatic series of streams and waterfalls. There's even a tropical aviary, and the latest addition is a seaquarium. Tours are held daily from 9 A.M. to 5 P.M. Admission is $10 per person.

Thirteen miles east of Ocho Rios is the village of Oracabessa. Watch for the Esso station. Take the narrow lane nearby leading toward the sea; you'll come upon a beach lined with old-style dugout canoes and gateposts topped by carved wood pineapples. This is **Golden Eye**, the villa owned for nearly two decades by Ian Fleming, author of the James Bond novels, and later by reggae legend Bob Marley. Other literary lights, including Truman Capote and Graham Greene, have escaped winter here. The villa is closed to the public.

While we're of a literary bent, let's proceed still farther eastward on the main coast road. Before reaching Port Maria, on your right, a sign directs you up a dirt road to the hilltop aerie of the late, great master of drawing-room wit—British playwright, author, and composer Noel Coward. Sir Noel's books, records, manuscripts, even his clothes closets are as he left them when he died in this simple house in 1973. Known as **Firefly** (no phone), it now belongs to the National Trust of Jamaica and is maintained as a museum and memorial. Coward's grave is behind his home, which is open daily, except Sunday, from 9 A.M. to 5 P.M.; admission is $1.75 for adults, 50 cents for children.

Route B13 from Port Maria leads to **Brimmer Hall** (994–2309), where you ride an open-air jitney through pimento (allspice), banana, and coconut groves. This working plantation has a great house for inspection, where a tasty lunch can also be had. It's open Monday through Saturday from 8 A.M. to 5 P.M.; admission is about $6.50 per person.

PORT ANTONIO

Beautiful and unspoiled, Port Antonio is still nearly the secret hideaway it once was for film stars Clara Bow, Bette Davis, Errol Flynn, and Ginger Rogers—not to mention J.P. Morgan, when he was the richest man in the world. Celebrities and an in-the-know elite continue to seek it out, but you don't have to be famous to share the wealth.

Possibly because this corner of Jamaica is difficult to get to—it's about a four-hour drive from MoBay and two hours from Kingston—Port Antonio has remained special and secluded. (You can, however, take an interisland flight from either city's airport to Ken Jones Airfield west of town.) But the effort is rewarded with a demure fishing village huddled around twin harbors, surrounded by Jamaica's lushest and most romantic countryside—and the chance to revel in what has been aptly described as "the most exquisite port on earth."

LODGING

Pleasant accommodations for the budget-minded are scarce in Port Antonio, but best is the **Bonnie View** (993–2752), Box 82, Port Antonio. On a street of the same name that begins in the center of town, this hilltop hotel offers spectacular views, an impressive pool and sundeck, and a restaurant that offers excellent home-style meals at a reasonable cost. While you dine you can watch the sun and an occasional storm cloud move in from Navy Island offshore to the village of Port Antonio sprawled below. This is the oldest, continuously operating hotel in the Caribbean, and while the passage of time shows, so does the loving care bestowed by managers Tony and Jane Wilson. There's horseback riding mornings and evenings, a lending library of paperback books and games, and 25 basic but clean rooms with small patios that run about $70, double, in-season.

Some three miles east of the village, on the coast road (Route A4), is the superb **Trident Villas and Hotel** (993–2602; toll-free 800–237–3237; in Miami, 305–666–3566; fax 809–993–2590); Box 119, Port Antonio. Trident is a dramatic cluster of villas, built by international architect Earl Levy, whose taste and professional savvy show in every manicured twist and turn. Go through a stone gate, and you're at the private beach where the chef stands ready to prepare his special Jerk chicken or fish. Six peacocks strut the hotel's lawns. A rounded, almost free-form swimming pool fronts the elegant Main House; tennis courts are lighted at night; 26 junior and villa suites, with personal maid and prompt room service, overlook the sea. Scuba diving and deep-sea fishing are quickly arranged. This paradise, however, can be costly: plan on $350 to $625 a night, double, including breakfast, afternoon tea, and dinner. (Off-season rates drop about 40%.)

In the evenings the candlelit dining room, which gleams with cut crystal, shining silver, and dress code (jacket and tie during the winter season, jacket only at other times), may be the best on the island, if not the entire Caribbean.

Breakfast can be taken (one course at a time) on your private balcony or veranda that faces the sea. Each of the 26 antique-furnished suites is distinctive and unique, with Jamaican-made replicas of antiques, ceiling fans to circulate sea breezes, a sitting room, and pantry with fridge and ice maker. Count on serenity—no TV or radio.

New to the neighborhood is the all-white **Jamaica Palace Hotel** built by the Baroness Siglinde von Stephani-Fahmi (she also started the castle later completed by Earl Levy). The all-white interior design, offset by black lacquer and gilded furniture, creates a Middle Eastern feeling in the 60 rooms and suites. All rooms have semicircular beds; there's a 114-foot swimming pool in the shape of Jamaica in an interior court. This one-of-a-kind hotel is priced at $100, double to $175 (plus 10% service charge and an additional $12 a day, room tax). Stop for a drink, and be sure to browse in the lobby boutique, which is owned by Patrice Wymore Flynn, the widow of Errol Flynn.

On a hill overlooking San San Bay about six miles east of Port Antonio, the villas at **Goblin Hill** (993–3286), San San, Port Antonio, are a tropical hideaway for couples or families who treasure the daily services of a cook and housekeeper in private villas with names like "Xanadu" and "La Mancha." White stucco buildings sit on sprawling, verdant grounds with glorious views of the bay. The beach is down the hill, and so it's a short drive to snorkeling and sand, but a pool is close at hand, as well as two night-lighted tennis courts. Other activities—water-skiing, scuba, horseback riding, and more—can be arranged. The dozen one-bedroom units go for $1,200 per week; the 16 two-bedrooms are about $1,750. All include airport transfers and a car.

In somewhat remote splendor, high atop a hillside, is the **Fern Hill Club** (993–3222; Toronto home office, 416–620–4666), Box 28, Port Antonio, some 45 acres carved out of limestone hills, with 46 units nestling into the cliffs. (Sturdy leg muscles are a plus here.) This is an all-inclusive with the accent on couples and families: four swimming pools, a lighted tennis court, evening entertainment, shuffleboard, table tennis, and water sports at San San beach (only scuba diving and horseback riding carry an extra charge). Best bet are the whirlpool spa suites, fully air-conditioned, split-level, decorated in muted pastels, with television (video on request) and small fridge. At all-inclusive rates ranging from $120 to $150 double, this is a find for those who don't mind the hilltop location.

EXPLORING

What's to see and do in Port Antonio? Well, you can explore the quaint village, enjoy the lush tropical green that all but envelopes you, or the beaches, or the sea—deep-sea fishing is excellent here. Many feel that one of the area's greatest charms is that it is largely unspoiled and un-developed, from a tourist's standpoint. So relax and enjoy.

Not that there aren't local sights worth finding. It's here, for example, that you can enjoy the best, and original, raft trip in Jamaica. Local lore has it that film star Errol Flynn started it all when he noticed the long, thin bamboo rafts being used to transport bananas down the Rio Grande River for shipping. Today, embarking from Berrydale, southwest of Port Antonio, a skilled raftman (and often a skilled storyteller) will guide you on an idyllic three-hour voyage to the sea; along the way, your two-passenger con-veyance may pause to allow you to splash in a quiet pool, or you can dangle a fishing line, or enjoy the picnic lunch you packed. Vendors sell Red Stripe beer and Cokes along the way—or you can hold out till you reach Rafters Rest, on St. Margaret's Bay at journey's end, where a bar, restaurant, and souvenir shopping await. The leisurely excursion costs about $35 per raft. For information, contact Rio Rafting (993–2626), 7 Harbour Street, Port Antonio.

East of Port Antonio's east harbor, on a headland, sits the remains of a vast classical structure known in the area as **Folly,** built in 1905 by a Connecticut jeweler named Alfred Mitchell. His wife was a Tiffany, and they lived here until Mitchell's death in 1912. Just east of the Trident Hotel, architect Earl Levy has worked for years to complete a fantasy castle that's now used as his country home (his office is in Kingston). Occasionally, fortunate guests at Trident Villas, his nearby hotel, are invited to drinks.

Just east of San San Bay, follow the signs to the **Blue Hole**—the Blue Lagoon, to those who saw the movie of the same name that was partially filmed here. More recently, this was the setting for another Hollywood tale, *Club Paradise.* Its intensely blue waters are estimated to reach down some 180 feet.

On a road that arcs south from Port Antonio and back to the coast at Fairy Hill are the caves of **Nonsuch,** popular with both serious spelunkers and the just plain adventuresome for their fossilized sea life, coral, and remnants of an early Arawak Indian community. Local guides are eager to help for a set fee of about $5, which includes a complimentary drink.

Near Priestman's River, a few miles east of Boston Bay —*the* place to sample jerk pork or chicken, an aromatic barbecue invented centuries ago by the freed slaves known as Maroons—lies the 2,000-acre ranch owned by Patrice Wymore Flynn.

The drive from Priestman's River along the coast (Route A4) to the town of Manchioneal is splendid—as scenic, many say, as the famed Hana Highway on the Hawaiian island of Maui. Just past Manchioneal, take the turnoff before the Driver's River bridge and detour inland for a mile or so until you reach a fork in the road. A crude sign will direct you to **Reach Falls**, one of the most spectacular waterfalls in all Jamaica—and one of the least visited. Stone stairs—watch your step!—lead to the bottom of the falls; then, if you wish, take a peak at the caves under the falls.

Kingston

This bustling metropolitan area of 700,000, most populous by far on the island and largest English-speaking city south of Miami, is often overlooked by vacationers. Savvy visitors, however, realize that coming to Jamaica and not visiting the capital of Kingston, is like visiting Mexico and not stopping off in Mexico City. You can certainly do it, but you miss the heart and soul of either country. It's estimated that only 5% of Jamaica's visitors come to Kingston. The capital since 1872, it is also the seat of island commerce and culture. The old pirate enclave of Port Royal is just across the harbor, and the beauty and serenity of the 7,000-foot Blue Mountains are a short drive away. By auto, Kingston is about four hours from Montego Bay, about two hours from Port Antonio, and under two from Ocho Rios.

The centerpiece of the capital these days is the area known as New Kingston, once a race track, and now a gleaming mix of hotels, restaurants, theaters, art galleries, reggae concerts by international superstars, hot clubs and bistros, movie theaters, music shops, jewelry stores, and interesting boutiques, as well as office towers and apartments. It is here that you will find the attractive Tourism Centre Building, at 21 Dominica Drive, home of the Jamaica

Tourist Board; it's your one-stop headquarters for answers or assistance regarding any locale or activity on the island.

This is tropical-style big city living, and while there's street crime (similar to other cities), there's also big city excitement.

LODGING

The city boasts several of the island's finest hotels. Remember that room rates listed here are in U.S. currency before tax and service charge (subject to fluctuations in the exchange rate, of course). Unlike the rest of Jamaica, where hotel rates are seasonal, Kingston rates remain the same the year-round.

Near the Tourism Centre Building is the **Wyndham Kingston** (926–5430; toll-free 800–822–4200), 85 Knutsford Boulevard. After a dazzling refurbishment by the Dallas-based Wyndham hotel group, it's become a solid hit with business and pleasure travelers alike. The first impression is tropical and expansive, with a lobby that is airy and accented with wicker and greenery. A 17-story tower and seven cabana buildings curl around the Olympic-sized pool and landscaped grounds, where macaws screech and the hubbub of the city is lost.

There's plenty to do here. Besides the pool, there's a health club, library, and tennis privileges at the night-lit Liguanea Club across the street. The hotel's top-floor Les Ambassadors Restaurant has just been revamped, with a new look and new menu, but no one changed the spectacular rooftop views of the city, the bay, and the mountains beyond. The breezy, open-air Cafe Macaw is perfect for a leisurely breakfast or lunch. In a party mood? Then head for the Jonkanoo Lounge.

The Wyndham has a total of 400 spacious rooms, all air-conditioned, though those in the tower are newer and afford the better views. Doubles range from $125 to $135, while those wanting the "ultraservice" of the "presidential" floors (14 through 16)—a private lounge and other extras— pay a double daily rate of $145 (with complimentary Continental breakfast and newspaper delivered to your door).

Practically next door is another splendidly renovated hostelry, the **Jamaica Pegasus** (926–3691; toll-free from the U.S. 800–225–5843), 81 Knutsford Boulevard. Here, the mood is elegant and upscale, with marble floors and pastel hues in the lobby, where you can find some of the best duty-free shopping on the island. Just off the lobby is the graceful Le Pavillion, noted for its afternoon teas, as well as elegant dining; and the Surrey Tavern, which serves up pub grub and, frequently, first-rate jazz, making it a popular Kingston nightspot.

Going up? The Talk of the Town, which sits atop the hotel on the 17th floor, has both city views and one of the most ambitious kitchens in town.

Going down? One level below the lobby is the pool bar and a dependable coffee shop, overlooking a sizeable kidney-shaped pool with a three-tiered fountain gurgling at one end. This is the setting for the weekly manager's cocktail party, replete with tasty island snacks, a bartender with a generous nature, and a lively calypso band. The pool and gardens are ringed by a jogger's track, and there is a health club, two new floodlit all-weather tennis courts, and a shallow children's pool. Inside, on pool level, there's an informal art gallery with some good canvases.

Each of the 350 attractively appointed rooms is air-conditioned, has satellite TV and a private balcony with a mountain or sea view. From the front desk attendant to the maid, the mood is helpful and efficient, and the 24-hour room service is fast and surprisingly reasonable (how about a pizza for about $3, or a steaming bowl of spicy Jamaican pepperpot soup for less than $1?).

Rates are about $135 to $145 for a double. The Pegasus is also a favored business address, and so its Knutsford Club floors (14 through 16) feature extras such as check-in facilities directly on the floor, private lounges, complimentary cocktail hours, and business services. Doubles here go for about $150, with a Continental breakfast and the morning *Gleaner* brought to your door.

At harborside, close to the convention center, National Gallery, and government offices, is another modern highrise, the **Hotel Oceana Kingston** (922–0920; toll-free 800–221–4588), 2 King Street. Built as a member of the Inter-Continental hotel chain, this is primarily a business and convention destination, though its splendid waterfront vista, pool, beauty salon, shopping arcade, and cocktail lounge with live entertainment make it a pleasurable stopover for anyone visiting the capital. The ferry to Port Royal across the bay is nearby, and the helpful hotel staff can also arrange for fishing, boating, or golf outings.

The 152 air-conditioned rooms all have TVs and are pleasantly appointed and modern. Ask for a harbor view. Double or single, they are $86 to $100; suites range from $110 to $500 per night.

The Courtleigh (926–8174), 31 Trafalgar Road, is a 72-room hostelry with the feel of a fine country club. Impeccable white buildings with well-tended greenery is the look without; white with accents of color predominates within. The pool area, with its umbrella-shaded tables and shingle-roofed bar, is especially restful. You are likely to meet visiting Britons here, sipping their gin and tonics and discussing cricket-league standings. The open-air Plantation Terrace hosts a civilized lunch, while a bar called Mingles is a favored evening destination. The Courtleigh's nicely appointed rooms start at around $74, with a three-bedroom suite costing $145.

Two erstwhile private residences offer a more homey stay. The **Mayfair** (926–1610), 4 West Kings House Close, is set on a lovely cul-de-sac near historic Devon House. The impressive main guest house has a pool and patio for use by all—as well as for locally renowned Wednesday and Saturday buffets—while the surrounding homes have been converted into rooms for hire.

This is a particular favorite of visitors from Britain and Europe, though hostess Sybil Hughes goes the extra mile to help all her guests enjoy both her hotel and the island. Expect to pay about $50 to $60 double occupancy; all guest rooms are air-conditioned and have private bath. You'll need to depend on taxis or a car to explore the city from here.

The main part of the **Terra Nova Hotel** (926–9334), 17 Waterloo Road, had its origins as a balustraded private home set amid manicured gardens. This five-acre property, including 32-room hotel, was recently bought by the Mutual Life Assurance Society, which is developing plans for refurbishment by the mid-1990s. The hotel and its restaurant

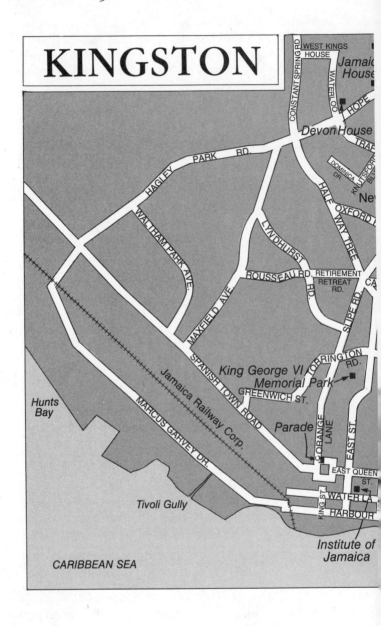

KINGSTON

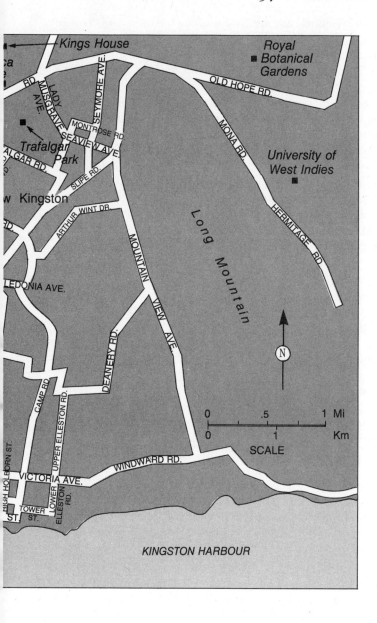

remain popular among the Jamaican business, government, and capital-society sets; after dark, its nightclub is a favorite spot among Kingstonian professionals. The rooms are all air-conditioned and the rate, single or double, is $70 to $85 per night. Since this hotel is also in a residential neighborhood, you'll need transportation to get around. How about a few days of splendid isolation? High above the city in the scenic Blue Mountains sits **Pine Grove Chalets** (922–8705); mailing address, 29 Olivier Place, Kingston. This is coffee-growing country, and this small lodge-like establishment is in the midst of a coffee plantation; it's refreshingly cool and lush up here, and the vistas are spectacular. In short, this is close to heaven for both lovers of solitude and lovers seeking solitude; many who stay here hike or climb the surrounding mountains.

The staff will prepare three delicious meals a day upon request—and the fare in the simple but attractive dining room or patio terrace, where the view is top-of-the-world, is both tasty and inexpensive. The 17 no-frills guest rooms all have refrigerators and cooking facilities, and televisions are available at extra charge; there are no phones in the rooms. Prices range from about $35 a night for a studio to only $40 for a one-bedroom cottage; extra beds are $2 apiece.

The 45-minute drive up from Kingston is not for the timid, because of the many mountain switchbacks and the rutted roadbed. Someone from the hotel will pick you up at the airport, if you make the arrangements in advance.

Finally, if even in a city as vibrant as Kingston you can't bear the thought of Jamaica without a beach, here's your solution: **Morgan's Harbour** (924–8464) on Main Road in Port Royal. The skyline of Kingston lies directly across the harbor, and is accessible in minutes by ferry. Norman Manley Airport is a short drive away; historic Port Royal, the ruined pirate enclave, is but a short hike. And the hotel itself is a port of call. Yachts bob in their berths just yards from the hotel's cafe and breeze-refreshed seaside bar—the hotel complex encompasses a yacht marina and beach club. Nearby is a cozy beach for sunning and salt-water swimming, and there's a harborside pool as well. Water-skiing, scuba, and deep-sea fishing are easily arranged.

The rooms are in two-story wings. Smallish but clean,

they are all air-conditioned and go for $78 to $170 a night, depending on the view.

EXPLORING

Kingston is chaotic and civilized. Kingston is exuberant and discreet. Kingston is tawdry and magnificent. Kingston is past and present. Above all, Kingston is the living heart of Jamaica—and no one who wishes to understand this fascinating people and place can overlook it.

The stunning contrasts of Jamaican culture can be seen in a few hour's tour along Hope Road just north of New Kingston. Start at **Devon House** (929–7029), at the intersection of Hope and Waterloo roads. This mansion—or great house, as these preserved architectural treasures are known on the island—dates to 1881; it was built by island craftsmen for George Stiebel, one of the first black millionaires of the West Indies, who furnished it elegantly with the best Caribbean-made pieces of his day. Both the historic house and its contents were restored to their original splendor for a visit by Queen Elizabeth II in 1983, and Devon House is today one of the country's best glimpses into a remarkable past. Open Tuesday through Saturday from 9:30 A.M. to 5 P.M.; admission is $1.75 for adults, about 75 cents for children.

A visit to Devon House isn't complete, however, without a stop out back, where the low buildings that form an enclosed courtyard formerly served as stables and a carriage house. Now they shelter the island's best collection of Jamaican crafts and gifts as a series of shops operated by Things Jamaican Ltd. There's also a tempting bakery and an ice-cream stand. (A scoop of guava or soursop, anyone?)

Sit on benches under the protective shade of a massive mahogany and admire the courtyard's profusion of tropical flora. Or better yet, step up onto the checkerboard-tiled back porch of the great house itself, settle into a wicker chair at one of the tables of **The Coffee Terrace** (929–7063), and treat yourself to a cool drink, a snack, or a full lunch, Monday through Saturday from 10 A.M. to 6:30 P.M.; Sunday brunch until 2:30 P.M.

A short distance east on Hope Road is a large park. Here, the modern **Jamaica House** was built in the 1960s as the residence of the prime minister, but today serves as the national leader's executive offices. (He lives close by on Montrose Road off Lady Musgrave Road, in a plantation house with a rooftop lookout tower that was built in 1694, known as Vale Royal.) Near the center of the park is **Kings House,** official residence of the governor-general, the British crown's representative on the island. Visitors may stroll the 200 acres of tranquil parkland, but neither house is open for touring.

Just beyond the park and its official buildings, at 56 Hope Road, is a startling sight. A walled 19th-century mansion over which an Ethiopian flag flies; through the ornate iron gate is clearly visible a massive figure in dreadlocks, a guitar slung across his chest. Welcome to the **Bob Marley Museum** (927–9152), a tribute to the reggae legend.

It was here that Marley lived with his wife and five children and recorded at a studio called Tuff Gong International. Today it continues to house the still-thriving Marley music empire, plus the most comprehensive collection of Marley memorabilia anywhere, documenting the musician's life from his ghetto childhood to worldwide acclaim to early death. The museum is open from 9:30 A.M. to 4:30 P.M. Monday, Tuesday, Thursday, and Friday; 12:30 to 5:30 P.M. Wednesday and Saturday. It closes for lunch hour at 1:30 P.M. Admission is about $2.50 for adults, $1 for children.

Back on Hope Road (which becomes Old Hope Road), the next stop is **Hope Botanical Gardens,** 200 acres laid out in the 1880s on land once belonging to Major Richard Hope, who arrived with the British in 1655. Since a visit by Queen Elizabeth II in 1953, these broad lawns and lovely ornamental gardens have been known officially as the Royal Botanical Gardens, though few Kingstonians call them that. Guides are on hand to give tours, but most of the tropical flora is labeled. The Orchid House is special. Children, especially, will like the small zoo and Coconut Park, a modest funland. Open daily 9 A.M. to 5 P.M.; free to all.

Another refuge from the hurly-burly of the city is the "You-wee" campus—the **University of the West Indies** —which extends both north and south of Old Hope Road past the botanical gardens. Its chapel, near the main entrance, is the biggest draw for visitors. "Edward Morant Gale: 1799" is inscribed at the top of the stone pediment below the roofline. Gale ran a sugar plantation in Trelawny, and this sturdy stone structure was his curing house; it was reassembled here, stone by stone. Much of the campus, in fact, sits on the site of the Mona and Papine sugarworks. Ruins of the aqueduct and sugar factory are scattered throughout the grounds.

Now head downtown, toward the waterfront. (A good route: Retracing your path, about a mile past the botanical gardens, is the intersection of Hope and Old Hope roads; take a left onto Old Hope; as you near downtown, this becomes Slipe Road.) At Torrington Road, a left will bring you quickly to **National Heroes Park,** formerly a race track and now nearly 75 acres of gardens, playing fields, and memorials to Jamaican heroes.

At the corner of Orange Street (the continuation of Slipe) and Ocean Boulevard, in the Roy West Building on the waterfront, is the new home of the **National Gallery of Jamaica** (922–1561). Opened here in 1984, the gallery houses a collection spanning the island's history from colonial times onward, but is particularly impressive in the works of Jamaicans since the 1920s. Several sculptures are on exhibit by Edna Manley, the talented wife of the nation's second prime minister. Also noteworthy are the sculpture (in the indigenous hardwood, lignum vitae) and painting of Mallica Reynolds, who called himself Kapo. Open Monday through Saturday, 10 A.M. to 5 P.M. Admission is free for students, $1 for adults.

A short jaunt westward is the recently refurbished **Jamaica Crafts Market** (922–3015), 52 Port Royal Street, the island's largest bazaar for handmade straw, wood, and embroidered goods—and a sightseeing stop in its own right. Many of these items are available nowhere else, so a look-see is worthwhile. Not much negotiating over price goes on here, except on more pricey items, but you may run a gauntlet of sidewalk higglers outside. Open Thursday through Tuesday, 8 A.M. to 5 P.M., Wednesday, 8 A.M. to 4 P.M.

The **Institute of Jamaica** (922–0620), 12 East Street, was founded in the 1870s "for the encouragement of literature, science, and art" and at this location houses the world's largest collection of West Indian reference material in the National Library of Jamaica, as well as a museum and herbarium in its Natural History Division. The library, indispensable for West Indian scholars, also contains intriguing oddities like the Shark Papers, damning evidence tossed overboard by a guilty sea captain and recovered years after in the belly of a shark. The natural-history collection includes everything from Arawak Indian carvings to living specimens of island plantlife. Open from 8:30 A.M. to 4:30 P.M. Monday through Thursday, 9 A.M. to 4 P.M. Friday, and 8:30 A.M. to 1 P.M. Saturday.

Across from the city, at the tip of the 17-mile-long spit of land that encloses Kingston harbor, lies what was once called the wickedest city in the world. In the late 17th century, **Port Royal,** home to pirate Henry Morgan and his Brethren of the Coast, was awash in booty robbed from Spanish galleons on the high seas. This was a party town— with 40 taverns to serve the lusty buccaneers and their innumerable ladies.

In 1692 a ruinous earthquake and tidal wave ended the party for good. But the port did not die. During the next century Port Royal served as West Indian headquarters for the British Royal Navy. It was during this period that a 20-year-old officer named Horatio Nelson, who would become a great admiral, was in charge of the 104 guns of Fort Charles, the oldest structure in Port Royal. Today it is a quiet fishing village with haunting echoes of its notorious past.

The old Naval Hospital at the fort is now the **Port Royal Archaeological and Historical Museum,** displaying centuries-old relics recovered by scuba expeditions from the submerged area of the pirate city just offshore. A small Maritime Museum is nearby, as is an old artillery store known as Giddy House, which stands at a tipsy angle thanks to a subsequent quake in 1907. St. Peter's Church, dating from 1754, boasts, in its collection of silver platters, a communion plate said to have been a gift from Morgan.

In a graveyard at the church entrance, one tombstone epitaph tells the strange-but-true tale of Lewis Galdy, "the man who died twice." The earth opened to swallow him in 1692, but another tremor spewed him into the sea, where he was rescued. "He lived many years after in Great Reputation," reads the stone; he died in 1739, at the age of 88.

All Port Royal attractions are open Monday through Saturday, 10 A.M. to 5 P.M.

The Inland Island

This is the Jamaica known by few but the Jamaicans themselves, the island without a beach (though the sea and sand are never very far away) but with a host of intriguing byways and all-but-undiscovered charms. If you want to know the "real" Jamaica, away from the cruise-ship ports and limbo contests, discover the Inland Island.

SPANISH TOWN

Although only a half-hour drive west from Kingston, the Inland Island starts here. Although there are no hotels we'd recommend, Spanish Town is a worthwhile stopover as you enter the Jamaican interior (or, driving down from Ocho Rios, as you approach Kingston). The city was originally laid out by a son of Christopher Columbus in the early 1500s; called Villa de la Vega, it served as the colonial capital for more than three centuries, until 1872.

Along the way are signs that introduce you to Jamaica in the present tense—RAM GOAT FOR SALE HERE, CHURCH

OF THE GOD OF PROPHECY, BIG MAMA PUB. There are also sights that remain frozen in memory—bottled honey and hanging fruits for sale from stands, a Rasta sitting by a wood shack wearing headphones, rocking to the silent music.

First, a bit of forewarning: Spanish Town is neither organized nor sanitized for the benefit of visitors. Streets are narrow and confusing, and are usually crowded with traffic and pedestrians. And despite its rich history, most of its residents are poor. If you lack a spirit of adventure, perhaps it would be wise to stick to a guided tour (available from Kingston or Ocho Rios) or skip this stop entirely.

EXPLORING

At the center of everything is the Plaza Mayor, the town square conceived by the Spanish, but bordered by architecture dating back only to British rule of the island. There's the old British House of Assembly (1762), with its long, shady colonnade, now used for local government offices; the grand portico and facade of King's House, once the governor's residence but gutted by fire in 1925; the 1819 courthouse; a cupolaed monument housing a marble statue of Admiral Rodney, the British naval commander who kept the French from seizing the island in 1782; as well as several historic Georgian houses.

A short, five-block walk back in the direction of Kingston brings you to the site of the oldest cathedral in the Western Hemisphere. The **Cathedral Church of St. James,** on Barrett Street, was originally constructed in 1523; the brick structure with wooden steeple that stands here now dates to 1714. Don't miss the tombs and memorials, some from the 17th century.

Three miles east of town, on Route A1 to Kingston, is the **White Marl Arawak Museum** (no phone), a reconstruction of an Arawak Indian hut on the site of a village from the island's pre-Columbian past. It's open from 10 A.M. to 5 P.M daily.

MANDEVILLE

Welcome to "alpine" Jamaica, 2,000 feet above the sea. Mandeville, population 13,600, is noted for its soft, cool climate. The island's "most English" city, it's also within easy striking distance of uncrowded, secluded south-coast beaches. Seventy-two miles from either Montego Bay or Ocho Rios, and 64 miles from Kingston, Mandeville is a wonderful change of pace.

LODGING

The Astra (962–3265), 62 Ward Avenue, Mandeville, is an 18-room, family-run inn in a residential area. What this hostelry lacks in resort-style amenities, it more than makes up for in friendliness and a willingness to please. More to the point, here's where to find Diana McIntyre-Pike, the enthusiastic hostess and Mandeville's biggest booster; if she doesn't have time to show you around town herself, she'll point you in all the right directions.

There is a 24-hour visitor information center here (the only one in town), as well as a pool, a sauna, a restaurant that serves up satisfying, homey Jamaican cuisine, and the popular Revival Pub. Horseback riding, golf, tennis, and excursions to local sights or Treasure Beach on the south coast can be arranged. If you book under the Modified American Plan (breakfast and dinner included), you can sample several area restaurants in addition to the Astra kitchen.

The inn's rooms range from about $50 to $100 per night double occupancy and some have kitchenettes. A package that includes dinner starts at about $75 per night.

You'll meet the rest of the McIntyre family at their flower-filled homestead, the **Mandeville Hotel** (962–2460 or 962–2138), Hotel Street. There are 60 rooms, some with kitchen facilities. Mark and Ceceline McIntyre purchased this historic hotel, originally built as the Waverly Hotel in 1875, in 1986. Now, son Gordon and his wife, Tel, add to the family feeling with their children, all contributing to the upkeep of rooms that are simply but nicely furnished. Double, with meals, range from $96 to $140, and of course, in this most English of Jamaican towns, there's complimentary afternoon tea.

EXPLORING

Crisp, clear air, mountain scenery, and the pleasures of the great outdoors are the major attractions in Mandeville and its environs. Temperatures hover in the 70s in winter, and averages 84° in summer. This is the garden and citrus center of the island, and the Jamaica Horticultural Society's show each summer is a microcosm of the best the island has to offer.

The town itself is orderly—you'll encounter no slums here, unlike elsewhere on the island—and has a tradition of wealth, thanks to its prominence as a bauxite-producing center. Many homes in the area are grand and imposing by anyone's standard. That certainly would describe the eight-sided mansion at 41 Manchester Road built by Cecil Charlton, a mayor of Mandeville for two decades—an indoor pool in the living room is connected to the outdoor swimming pool by an underground tunnel. Your hotel can make touring arrangements for everyday except Wednesday and Saturday; no charge, but donations will go to a local charity.

Mandeville's epicenter is the traditional town green, where you'll find a Georgian courthouse and a pretty parish church of native stone. But for the best view of the town and the surrounding countryside, stop at the 150-year-old former hotel that is now **Bill Laurie's Steak House** (962–3116) in Bloomfield Gardens. A collection of antique cars that were the pride of the late Mr. Laurie, sits out front. Enid Laurie, who is also the cook, intends to carry on the Laurie tradition, which emphasizes imported steaks, strong punches, and unbeatable views.

Not far from the Hotel Astra is **Marshall's Pen,** built about 1795, a magnificent great house on acres of rolling countryside. The house and land have been in the Sutton family for more than 50 years, and it's their pleasure to show visitors their treasured silver pieces and colonial furniture. To date, patriarch Robert Sutton has catalogued some 89 species of birds, and he welcomes other dedicated bird fanciers by appointment through the Astra Hotel (962–2260). The 300-acre property remains a working cattle farm.

Northeast of town, where Routes B4, B5, and B6 converge, is Shooter's Hill. Alcan, the Canadian Aluminum Corporation, has its **Kirkvine Works** (962–3141) nearby—look for the red bauxite "lake" at the foot of the hill. Weekday tours can usually be arranged with a day's notice. Atop the hill is the tomb of the man who once owned this piece of real estate, Alexander Woodburn Heron; the Blue Mountain Peak, 60 miles distant, can be seen from this vantage point on clear days.

But to gourmet-shop devotees the most important stop at Shooter's Hill is the **Pickapeppa Factory** (962–2928), home to the famed piquant sauce that is sold worldwide; call ahead to see if a tour can be arranged.

Two more factory tours of note: The **High Mountain Coffee Factory** (962–4211) in the nearby town of Williamsfield, where Jamaica's exalted beans (including the renowned Blue Mountain) are processed and packed, can be toured weekdays by prior arrangement by phone or through your hotel. The same is true for the **Pioneer Chocolate Company** (962–4216), also in Williamsfield.

Even those not overly interested in gardens fall under the spell of **Mrs. Carmen Stephenson** (962–2328), 25 New Green Road. This charming lady has won countless prizes in the annual Horticultural Show and grows almost every species of orchid, including an almost black orchid. Her pin-neat property is also loaded with citrus trees, and she'll sell you a bag of whatever is in season at the lowest cost anywhere. A requested donation for the complete tour is about $1.50.

One of our favorite "finds" in Jamaica is the **1907 Gallery,** which will take a bit of effort for outsiders to locate. Stick with it, and ask directions until you find **1907 Caledonia Meadows** (962–0109). As you enter this gallery-cum-bar, you may be confused at first. Every piece is a collectible, carefully put in place by John Deer, who scours the countryside for his finds. Everything, including the antique bed, is for sale. Sit on a century-old barber chair (one of four) at his bar and listen to the owner's story.

Charles Swaby takes guests on personalized tours along Jamaica's longest river, the Black River, which makes a 44-mile journey to the sea. Give him a call in Mandeville at 2 Newleigh Boulevard (962–0220), or at High Street in Black River (965–2513). There are some 100 species of birds in this 16,000-acre wetland, which is also the breeding ground of the endangered American crocodile and game fish such as snook, tarpon, and mullet.

Sports—Sun & Fun

This is why you choose sunny Jamaica over, say, the Yukon —right? The sun. The sea. The sun. The golf. The sun. The tennis. The sun. And so on.

The great outdoors in the Caribbean—it doesn't get much better than this. We've hunted up the most fun you can have in the sun, and arranged it all alphabetically by category for easy reference. Spectator sports are covered at the end of the chapter. All prices listed are in U.S. currency.

BEST BEACHES

If "life is a beach," as the bumper sticker seen often back in the U.S.A. proclaims, then Jamaica is really *living*. We're talking about 200 miles of fine, soft, white sand, from cozy secluded coves to stretches that extend past the horizon.

Unless you're staying in Kingston—which is on the water but not on a beach—or in Mandeville—in the hilly interior—chances are that your hotel will either have its own private patch of sand, or access to one. Still, whether it's for privacy or a party scene or a place to broil *au naturel,* there are beaches in Jamaica definitely worth seeking out.

In general, the island's best beaches are on the north shore. In peak season, these are also the most likely to resemble Fort Lauderdale on spring break—especially around the most popular resorts of Montego Bay and Ocho Rios. Of the public beaches, most celebrated by far is **Doctor's Cave Beach** in Montego Bay. Popular with Jamaicans and visitors alike, this famed five-acre stretch of sugary sand has been the subject of countless travel articles and brochures over the years, all of which have contributed to its present status as the island's No. 1 sunning spot. Changing rooms are available. Vendors roam its length, and there is no lack of snacking opportunities nearby.

Surplus sun worshippers from Doctor's Cave often head up the coast to smaller **Cornwall Beach.** There's plenty of action here, too, as well as innumerable chances to find food and drink nearby. To the south, on the bay and very near the center of town, **Walter Fletcher Beach** offers another option: the protection of the bay affords unusually fine swimming.

In Ocho Rios, the "happening" beach is **Mallard's,** with the Mallards Beach and Americana hotels, and various shops, bars, and restaurants galore, close at hand. But **Turtle Beach,** to the south along the bay, is public sand that is enjoyed by both islanders and tourists.

Other North-Coast public beaches worth trying include **Puerto Seco** at Discovery Bay; and **San San** and **Boston Beach** (*the* place for "jerk pork") in Port Antonio. Ah, but for Jamaica's ultimate beach, head for the seven-mile-long strip of white sand at **Negril.**

Looking for uncrowded *and* undiscovered? Jamaica's south shore is little known to tourists, but that's simply because it has yet to be developed sufficiently to attract them. At these beaches you're only likely to encounter Jamaicans, and that alone makes them interesting and special. **Bluefields Beach,** near Savanna-la-Mar south of Negril, is quiet, and **Crane Beach** at Black River is both serene and scenic. It's another 20 miles along the coast (or about an hour's drive down from Mandeville) to **Treasure Beach,** the best beach on the south shore.

Kingstonians sometimes travel some 32 miles east to **Lyssons Beach** in Morant Bay, but usually favor other choices closer to home. Chief among these are the black-sand beaches of **Fort Clarence** in the Hellshire Hills area southwest of the city, which offer both changing facilities and frequent entertainment, including reggae; and the even better **Naggo Head,** where rich and poor coexist in *irie* harmony. Another best bet: For a small, negotiable fee, you can hire a boat at the marina of Morgan's Harbour near Port Royal to ferry you to nearby **Lime Cay,** an island just beyond Kingston Harbour, for several hours of picnicking, sunning, and swimming.

Finally, back to Negril, the island's mecca for the uninhibited. Although Jamaicans themselves are rather reserved when it comes to nudity, it's commonplace at **Negril Beach** for visiting female sun worshippers to go topless. At the Hedonism II resort and at its neighbor resort, the Grand Lido, beaches are reserved for nude sunbathing. Take-it-all-off tanning is also permitted at the private beaches of **Sandals** in Montego Bay, **Jamaica Jamaica** at Runaway Bay, and **Couples** in Ocho Rios.

Boating

Many resorts offer small sailboats—Sunfish and Sailfish —for use free of charge by their guests; others charge roughly $10 an hour. Chartering larger craft for cruising or sailing is easy, except for bare-boat charters, which are harder but not impossible to find. Contact one of the following: in the Kingston area, the **Royal Jamaica Yacht Club** (924–8685) or **Morgan's Harbour Marina** (924–8464), which also berths visiting yachts; in MoBay, the **Montego Bay Yacht Club** (952–3028).

Water Sports Enterprises (974–2185) in Ocho Rios offers yacht excursions to Dunn's River Falls for about $15 per person, including drinks and dancing on the beach. From the harbor at Port Antonio, the *Lady Jamaica* cruises for an hour or so at about $5 per person; there's a longer sail that includes drinks and a snack for $10. Make reservations through your hotel.

CAMPING, CLIMBING, AND HIKING

The Jamaica Alternative Tourism, Camping & Hiking Association (JACHA), c/o Arthur's Golden Sunset Restaurant (957–4241), Norman Manley Boulevard, Negril, sets up camping and guest-house accommodations, as well as backpacking, biking, climbing, hiking, and river-canoeing trips.

Ever tried waterfall climbing? The most popular, but not the most challenging, hike in Jamaica is the 600-foot climb to the top of Dunn's River Falls near Ocho Rios. It's a wet adventure best done in a bathing suit; changing facilities are provided, and the climb costs about 50 cents per person, plus a guide (optional) to point out the slippery spots and snap your photo. The Nonsuch Caves south of Port Antonio offer both amateur and more serious adventurers interesting fossils, coral, and relics of a long-gone Arawak Indian settlement.

Hiking possibilities abound in the hills above the north-shore coastline, in the environs of Mandeville, and in the Blue Mountains in the southeastern part of the island. Serious climbers who wish to scale all or part of the 7,402-foot Blue Mountain Peak should contact the Jamaica Tourist Board (929–9200) for info on the series of mountain camps maintained by government foresters.

CYCLING

What better way to explore and enjoy the Jamaican coastline? Bicycles are loaned out by many hotels, and in Montego Bay, Ocho Rios, and Negril bike rentals are easy to find near the beaches and are inexpensive—about $8 a day. A ride to Dunn's River Falls or Fern Gully in the Ocho Rios area, to Rose Hall near Montego Bay, or along the seven-mile strip of Negril beach, is a particularly fine excursion.

Less of a workout but more exhilarating is to make the trip on a moped, motor scooter, or small motorcycle. Mopeds and scooters are available through many hotels and some rental agencies at $20 or more per day. **Stony Hill Castle Ltd. Bike Rentals** has locations in Montego Bay (953–2292), Ocho Rios (974–2681), and Negril (957–4460); and rents Honda 185 Trail bikes and CM200 Twin Stars at $50 a day; a Honda C50 Scooter is $25 per day. There are three-day and weekly rates as well; gasoline is extra. A deposit (or credit-card voucher) and a valid driver's license are required.

FISHING

You've come to the right place. The freshwater catch from the island's rivers can be abundant, and the deep-sea bounty is often downright spectacular. No license is needed to try either.

Some of the edible river dwellers here include drummer, mullet, snook, and tarpon. If you want a go at them, remember to bring your own tackle. Or, if you go river rafting on the Martha Brae River near Falmouth or the Rio Grande in Port Antonio, the raftsman will give you a baited line to dangle out.

Salt-water charters are most easily booked through your hotel, though a harborside stroll might land a better price, if your luck is good and the captain wants your business. Prices begin at about $450 for a full day, $225 for a half day, which includes boat, crew, tackle, and bait; some boats will take you aboard on a shared charter at around $75 a day, $55 a half day.

Port Antonio, especially, is known for some of the best deep-sea fishing in the Caribbean, but charters are also popular from Kingston, Ocho Rios, and, to a lesser extent,

Negril. Blue and white marlin are the main attractions, and late summer and early winter are the best times to bait your hooks. Other challenging possibilities include barracuda, bonita, dolphin (*not* the Flipper kind), kingfish, sailfish, tuna (Allison and yellowfin), and wahoo.

Spearfishing, legal along the reefs, can produce any number of species, including grouper, jack, mackerel, snapper, and tarpon. Bring your own gear.

GOLF

As you would expect of a nation with links to Great Britain (pardon the pun), golf is almost a religion here, with courses, pros, caddies, and greenskeepers to match any in the Caribbean. Greens fees in winter range from about $15 to $45 for 18 holes. And, unlike back home, it's usually cheaper—and certainly more instructive—to hire a caddy than to rent a cart; the former asks about $15 or less for 18 holes, the latter can cost upward of $25. For the fun of it, play at least a round or two with the smaller British ball and gloat over the extra distance in your drives.

Altogether, the island boasts nine courses, all with challenging holes and breathtaking vistas. Four of these are near Montego Bay. Though all are on hotel grounds, you don't have to be a guest to play. Unless otherwise specified, all have carts, caddies, and clubs for hire.

Tryall (952–5110), at the first-class resort of the same name, is a PGA Tour approved course with gorgeous links parallel to the sea. **Ironshore Golf Club** (953–2800) is characterized by beautifully kept fairways, lush greens, and several lakes. **Half Moon** (953–2280) is part of the ultra-plush resort complex of the same name, and this dandy 18-holer was designed by Robert Trent Jones. Last but definitely not least is what *Golf Digest* termed "the most remarkable combination of highland, linksland, and crazy golf," **Wyndham Rose Hall** (933–2650).

In Ocho Rios, **Upton Golf Club** (974–2528) is nestled into the rolling countryside above town. It's worth playing the first nine just to play the tenth, with its sweeping panorama of the Caribbean. A few miles east along the coast, **Runaway Bay Golf Club** (973–2561) was laid out by James Harris, a British naval commander and golfing purist; it's a thinking golfer's course and the site of the annual Jamaica Open, which is held each November.

Manchester Club (962–2403) in Mandeville is the island's oldest course. Though it has only nine greens, its 18 tees allow each green to double up, as it were. Lush and green at more than 2,000 feet above sea level, the vistas here are especially fine. No carts are available, but caddies and clubs are on hand.

In Kingston, tricky **Caymanas Golf Club** (926–8144) hosts the Red Stripe Invitational Tournament with celebrity players. No carts, but caddies and a limited supply of clubs can be rented. In a hilly northern suburb, **Constant Spring** (924–1610) is short, tight, and challenging. There are no carts, but caddies and clubs are available.

Horseback Riding

A sense of Jamaica's past can be had on horseback, since many of the best riding opportunities are on historic plantations or ranches. Or, in the case of **Chukka Cove Farms** (972–2506) on the former Llandovery estate west of Ocho Rios, there's an echo of the island's colonial tie to Great Britain. Polo instruction, anyone? How about jumping and dressage? This is one of the finest equestrian centers in the West Indies, and it leads picnic, trail, and moonlight rides at about $25 an hour per person. There's a choice of riding classes, half- to full-day trail and picnic rides, two- and three-day treks into the hills for about $80 per person, and one-hour rides at about $20. It's also the setting for polo action on Thursday and Saturday or Sunday afternoons. Check the local *Gleaner* for precise times.

Guided rides elsewhere in Ocho Rios are at **Prospect Estates** (974–2058); in Montego Bay, **White Witch Stables** (953–2746); and in Negril, **Hedonism II** (957–4200). At any of the above, the going rate is roughly $20 an hour.

PARASAILING

Ride that giant kite tethered to a speeding power boat —up, up, you climb until you are like a huge, multicolored bird against the deep blue sky! Parasailing is undeniably a thrill, and one you can experience in Negril, Montego Bay, and Ocho Rios. Figure on about $15 for a 25-minute soar. Ask at your hotel to find the local parasailing action.

RIVER RAFTING

Swashbuckling Errol Flynn, the Forties film star, is said to have invented this only-in-Jamaica adventure when he decided that the long, thin bamboo rafts used by the islanders to transport bananas could ferry passengers equally as well. Today, there are four separate rafting trips available in Jamaica; the original at Port Antonio, a shorter trip at Falmouth, one on the White River in Ocho Rios, and another through the Mountain Valley near MoBay.

The best, and original, rafting is on the Rio Grande, starting at Berridale (952–0889) south of Port Antonio; the leisurely three-hour trip to the sea costs about $35 per raft. A shorter trip down the Martha Brae River starts south of Falmouth (west of MoBay) and costs about $30 for two; your hotel will also book reservations.

There's rafting on the White River at Ocho Rios run by the folks from **Calypso Rafting** (974–2527). It's about a 45-minute trip through jungle foliage, at $25 per two-person raft. The latest entry, an hour trip run by **Mountain Valley Rafting** (952–0527), picks up guests at MoBay hotels and uses two-person rafts ($26) to glide silently along the shores of Lethe Village. Serious devotees will take all four trips.

Scuba and Snorkeling

Jamaica underwater is, if anything, more fascinating than it is above-sea-level. The clear, warm waters of the Caribbean invite snorkelers and divers to explore the rainbow-hued coral reefs and volcanic shoals—and they are rewarded by brightly colored fish and gently swaying sea flora. At depths of 100 feet or less, divers can hunt centuries-old shipwrecks and photograph larger, even more dramatic marine life.

Almost every area on the north shore harbors its own sea scenery. Kingston harbor, because of its long history of ocean-crossing traffic and pirate past, is a favorite among divers.

Several hotels, especially the all-inclusives, offer snorkel gear, as well as scuba instruction and a free tank a day as part of the package. To rent scuba gear or participate in guided scuba trips from a dive shop, you must show a certification card—unless you sign up for an instruction course.

A one-tank scuba trip costs upwards of $35 (off a boat), with a certified diving instructor and all equipment; snorkel trips run roughly $15. Scuba instruction—three hours in a pool and a one-tank dive in open water—costs $60 or more.

Among reputable dive shops that rent scuba and snorkel gear and lead guided trips are: In Montego Bay, **Seaworld,** with branches at four MoBay hotels (953–2180), **North Coast Marine Sports** at Half Moon (953–2211), and **Poseidon Nimrod Divers** (952–3624). In the Ocho Rios area, **Island Dive Shop** (972–2519), **Sea and Dive Jamaica** (974–5762), and **Water Sports Enterprises** (974–2185). In Negril, **Aqua Nova** (957–4323), **Negril Scuba Center** (357–4425), **Blue Whale** (957–4438), **Mariner's Inn Scuba Center** (957–4348), and **Sun Divers Ltd.** (973–2346).

SURF'S UP!

Though not noted for the power of its surf, Jamaica isn't without its tubular thrills. Head for Boston Bay, east of Port Antonio on the north shore, where the waves are as near to perfect as anywhere on the island.

TENNIS

This is another game Jamaicans take seriously. They play early in the morning or on night-lit courts to avoid the sizzle of the Caribbean sun—and you should do likewise unless you are in exceptional shape or the thermometer registers in the mid-70s or lower. Heat and humidity can take a quick toll on the unwary.

The good news is that there are lots of courts—more than 130 across the island, with the greatest concentration in MoBay and Ocho Rios. Nearly every major hotel has at least one, and nonguests can usually play for a court fee of about $10 per person an hour; guests play for free. Several resorts also have resident pros and clubhouses.

Do try to remember to bring an extra can or two of tennis balls if you intend to play often. Like many imported items, they're expensive here.

WATERSKIING

Though it is offered free to guests at many hotels, this popular water sport can cost roughly $1 a minute or about $25 for a half-hour of wave slicing. The Blue Lagoon in Port Antonio and Doctor's Cave Beach in Montego Bay are two popular places to slice across the water on skis.

Jet skiing is another speedy alternative. Skis can be

rented—about $20 for half an hour—at Cornwall Beach in MoBay and Turtle Beach in Ocho Rios.

WINDSURFING

Devotees of windsurfing—it's also called sailboarding —can catch the wind in their sails at any number of hotel beaches, where this sport is offered as part of the activities program. Instruction is also commonly available. It's a great spectator sport, too, watching the experts twist and turn and perform incredible acrobatics.

SPECTATOR SPORTS

Do you like to watch? When it comes to organized sports, things are very British here. Cricket is the national mania, and international matches—"tests"—are played from January through August in Sabina Park, Kingston. Soccer—it's called football here—runs a close second. The season begins in the fall and runs through the winter; check the *Daily Gleaner* for information about matches, or ask at your hotel or the nearest Jamaica Tourist Bureau office.

And then there's polo. This sport of kings is played on Saturdays throughout the year at Drax Hall, five miles west of Ocho Rios; and on Thursdays and Sundays at Caymanas Park, in a western suburb of Kingston. The ever-expanding equestrian center at Chukka Cove Farm in Ocho Rios has really put polo on the visitor's program. At about 4 P.M. on Thursdays and Saturdays, there's usually polo of some sort going on (call 972–2506 to be sure). Events range from "family games" to high-goal polo with Palm Beach players.

Restaurants

Adapting Jamaica's motto slightly, it becomes: "Out of many, one cuisine." Indeed, from a cultural stew begun centuries ago that has come to include Arawak Indian, Spanish, African, English, East Indian, Chinese, Syrian, and more, flavors have emerged that, while related to those found elsewhere in the Caribbean and the world, are at the same time distinctly Jamaican.

While there is no lack of more familiar fare—including Continental, Italian, and Chinese cuisine, broiled fresh seafood, even, yes, fast-food burgers and fried chicken—don't pass up the opportunity to eat as the Jamaicans do. Especially if you enjoy food on the spicy side, you will discover much to love here.

Soups, in particular, are akin to a folk art. Pepperpot is thick and meaty and, despite its name, will warm you without setting you afire; it's made from salt pork, beef, okra, coconut milk, and callaloo, a local leafy vegetable. Other delights include fish "tea," conch soup (made from the mullosk whose beautiful shell is sold to tourists along the north shore), red pea, and pumpkin.

Ackee and saltfish are part of every traditional Jamaican breakfast (but, as the national dish, is also served at other times)—it's cod; an exotic fruit brought to the island by the notorious Captain Bligh that tastes remarkably like scrambled eggs when baked; onions; and slices of hot peppers. An acquired taste for many, but worth a try.

Curries, hot and flavorful, are common. Curried goat is a popular main dish; have it with the excellent Jamaican mango chutney. Other local favorites that shouldn't be missed: roast suckling pig, rice and peas (kidney beans, actually, and cooked in coconut milk), stamp and go (spicy cod fritters). Patties—tasty pastries filled with ground beef, breadcrumbs, onion, and lively seasonings—are everywhere in Jamaica, the national snack or lunch.

A few words about jerk pork, jerk chicken, and jerk fish. They're all sensational, if you like barbecue. "Jerk" is derived from a Spanish word of Indian origin, and means to prepare pork (the only *authentic* jerked meat, though chicken and fish are equally delicious) in the manner of the Quechua Indians of South America. The method of slow cooking over a fire of green pimento wood was thought to have been learned by the Arawaks of Jamaica, passed to the Maroons—the freed slaves of the Spanish colonialists— then adopted by the rest of the island by the 19th century. Today you'll find roadside purveyors of this special treat throughout the island, especially along the North Coast, but devotees insist the very best is to be found along the beach at Boston Bay, east of Port Antonio.

Need something cooling after the tang of jerk pork or a patty? Jamaican fruit is excellent, from the familiar banana, coconut, orange, and pineapple to the more exotic guava, mango, passion fruit, pawpaw (papaya), rose apples, and soursop. From February to April, in the star-apple season, look for a salad dish called "matrimony," a sensuous marriage of star apples, either green-skinned or purple, oranges, milk, nutmeg, and sugar. Native fruits also make delectable tarts and ice creams.

Thirsty? Blue Mountain coffee is revered by gourmands everywhere, and Jamaican rum is some of the world's finest. Myers and Appleton rums, white or dark, have a longstanding rivalry as the island's best. So-called "overproof" rum, available under various labels, is favored by many locals; it has a taste all its own, but is extremely potent.

Tia Maria, the coffee liqueur, is also a native product, as is the lesser-known Rumona, a rum liqueur. Sangster's Old Jamaica liqueurs come in five varieties (and lovely ceramic bottles), including Blue Mountain Coffee and Orantique, a unique hybrid of orange and tangerine.

Red Stripe beer, the island brew, is likewise excellent. Not to be forgotten, Jamaican water is not only perfectly fine to drink, but it tastes good as well.

One offering that is *not* perfectly fine to drink is mushroom tea. Especially in Negril, you'll come across places that sell this dangerous concoction made from psylicybin, or "magic," mushrooms. It may produce hallucinations.

Dining out in Jamaica is not typically a dressy affair— only those establishments in the upscale resorts of the North Coast and the better restaurants of Kingston require that men wear a jacket and tie to dinner—but except for the most laid-back, beachside eatery, bare feet and bikinis aren't acceptable either.

The establishments listed below offer some of Jamaica's very finest eating. Arranged by location, they accept all major credit cards unless otherwise noted. Remember that many restaurants add a 10 percent gratuity to the check. Prices quoted are in U.S. currency.

NEGRIL

This is a place of serendipity. Some of the best meals you find here will be the lucky discovery of the tiny hole-in-the-wall, the thatched-roof snack bar, the Rastaman barbecuing chicken by the roadside. In this category falls **Desi's Dread** (no phone), at Negril Craft Park, is a true find. George Clarke has recently taken over from his famed Rasta brother Desmond and continues to serve only natural vegetarian foods and juices (soursop, carrot, banana, peanut beet root, and combinations thereof). Dishes, stewed or steamed on coal pots in back, are spooned into carved calabash bowls with wooden spoons. Rasta posters cover the shack walls, all painted in Rasta colors (red, yellow, green). Cost is minimal. Open 9 A.M. to 7 P.M.

But there are well-known, even famous, places, too. Chief among these is **Rick's Cafe** (957–4335), also on the lighthouse road. They say Rick's is perched on the western-most promontory in Jamaica; it certainly has no peers when it comes to sunset watching . . . or watching the sunset watchers. It's *the* meet 'n' greet spot in Negril. Reaching Rick's was once quite an ordeal, but now the road is paved, and the tour buses make the trip regularly. But you can still dive off the craggy rocks into the incredibly blue-green sea below. Be forewarned: It's noisy, crowded, and very popular.

You order at the blackboard before being seated on the open-air terrace overlooking the sea below. Dinner could range from a mixed grill of fresh fish ($12) to steamed shrimp with lime (about $22) or one of the more moderate entrees in the $7 neighborhood. Open daily from noon to 10 P.M. No credit cards.

A lunch and dinner favorite among *real* folk (those who live here), as well as visitors, is **Cosmo's Sea Food Restaurant and Bar** (957–4330), on Norman Manley Boulevard, a big name for a big place. Polished wooden family-style tables and benches are scattered inside this open-air favorite, owned and run by Cosmos Brown. The restaurant closes only from 5 to 6:30 P.M.; otherwise, it has continuous service of curry goat, stew pork, chicken and chips, fish and chips, and grilled or curry lobster, at prices that average $8. Conch soup, the specialty, is a meal in itself. This is a place to come in a bathing suit (with coverup), for ocean dips between courses.

"Informal but elegant" is both the dress code and mood at the **Charela Inn** (957–4277), less than a mile north of town on Norman Manley Boulevard. Five-course dinners combining French and Jamaican cuisine are served with down-home aplomb here—entrees like lobster Creole and stuffed baked crab—on the outdoor patio by the beach or in the classy indoor dining room. About $20 per person before drinks. The patio is perfect for a leisurely breakfast or lunch. Open daily from 8 A.M. to 10 P.M.

MONTEGO BAY

The **Calabash** (952–3891), 5 Queen's Drive, has both a superb view of the bay below and some of the finest seafood and Jamaican cooking in MoBay. Look for the blue awning marking the entrance in the Winged Victory Hotel. A casual dinner house, the Calabash's tasty specialty is a combo of baked crabmeat, lobster, shrimp, and white fish in a blue-cheese-and-brandy sauce. Also recommended is the spicey pork. And if tropical drinks appeal, don't miss their "house" mix of rum, liqueurs, and juices. The cost is about $20 per person, without drinks or wine. Open 7:30 A.M. to 11 P.M. daily.

A few steps down Queen's Drive stands a stately colonial mansion turned restaurant that has become a place to be seen as much as a place to dine. **The Diplomat** (952–3353) affords an equally stunning view of the ultramarine sea. Steaks, fresh seafood, and international fare—but it's the ambience and setting that makes it worth $25 or more per diner. Open for dinner daily, except Sunday. It's popular, so reservations are a good idea.

Less fancy, less expensive, but no less popular is **The Wexford Grill** (952–2854), 39 Gloucester Avenue, not far from Doctor's Cave Beach. It's in a porchlike section of the Wexford Hotel (which actually fronts a small street off Gloucester called Corniche Court), and it's the real thing, Jamaica-style. Huge portions of curried goat, chicken fricassee, and fresh fish as well as baked-on-premises cakes and pies are some of the highlights. Prices are quite reasonable —$10 per person should do it for dinner. Open daily for breakfast, lunch, and dinner. American Express only.

Across Gloucester Avenue from the Coral Cliff Hotel and right at water's edge is a jewel of a place called **Marguerite's by the Sea** (952–4777). They'll provide free transportation to and from most hotels, and once there, diners can choose between the seaside terrace or the attractive indoor dining room. Either way, the service is professional, and the food reliably good to excellent. Try the lobster sauté flamed with brandy or the "daily Caribbean catch" steamed in coconut milk. About $25 per person for dinner, and worth it. Open for dinner daily.

In the thick of historic MoBay, the **Town House** (952–2660), 16 Church Street, was built in 1765, a decade before the old Parish Church which stands across from it was built. A host of visiting celebs, including Paul McCartney, Dustin Hoffman, and the Duke of Marlborough, have broken bread here over the years. The fare is a pleasing assortment of Jamaican (smoked marlin, pumpkin soup), Continental (red snapper mornay), American (steak, spare ribs), and fresh seafood (steamed yellow tail, broiled lobster). Entrees range from $15 to $25. Open for lunch and dinner; dinner only Sundays. Free pick-up service from your hotel.

On a hill above town, the **Richmond Hill** (952–3859) is a wonderfully romantic great house built in the 1700s that has been converted to a small inn and restaurant. The views are delightful, especially at night, as you dine by candlelight on an open-air terrace near the pool. The steaks and lobster are first-rate, but chicken lovers will go for the house preparation of boneless breasts stuffed with spinach and topped with a cream sauce. Dinner entrees start at $25, at lunch, $10 and up. Open daily. Courtesy round-trip transportation is provided.

Two special splurges are recommended at MoBay-area resorts. The first is at **Tryall Golf and Beach Club** (952–5110), a dozen miles west of town on the coast highway, Route A1. On a terrace of the superb great house that commands the hillside, you dine under the stars—anything from a thick steak to the chef's own Jamaica-style paella—drink from the extensive wine list, then cap the evening off with dancing and entertainment. On Monday nights you can enjoy a vast seafood buffet, and on Fridays, a beach barbecue and native floor show. Figure at least $35 or more per person, without drinks or wine. Jackets required for gentlemen; reservations a must. Dinner nightly from November through mid-May only.

The other special evening awaits at the **Sugar Mill Restaurant** (953–2228) of the swank Half Moon Club, seven miles east of town on Route A1. There's a picturesque waterwheel as you enter, and dining is on the candlelit patio. The kitchen is creative, with the emphasis on Caribbean cuisine and fresh seafood: grilled lobster with fresh asparagus, mushrooms, tomatoes, plantains, carrots, cauliflower, broccoli, beans, and root vegetables of all description; Jamaica's most elegantly served Jerk pork, chicken and fish; and many pastas, including fettucine with smoked marlin. There are more than 100 wines from Europe and the United States, and delightfully decadent deserts. Plan on spending about $12 to $30 per person here, or at their adjacent **Seagrape Terrace** (953–2212). This terrace, fronted by the sea, concentrates on imported meat fillets (surf and turf) and imaginative cooking such as boneless chicken breast with shredded coconut. Bring money and wear your newest designer duds.

OCHO RIOS

A moveable feast in Ocho would proceed along Main Street, and a great place to start is the **Almond Tree** (974–2813) on the seaside back patio of the Hibiscus Lodge (near the Catholic Church). Your visit should begin in the bar, where the "stools" are swinging chairs; actually, it may have to, because this is a busy place in high season, and even those with reservations often wait for their tables with an Almond Tree Delight—a house drink made of rums, cherry liqueur, strawberry, oranges and lime juices. Dinner is best here, with its candlelit views of the Caribbean and an extensive menu that includes fondue bourguinonne, steak Diane, and crabmeat Milanese. Expect to pay $22 or more per person before drinks. Open daily for lunch and dinner.

Sleek and chic is **Le Gourmand** (972–2717), at Coconut Grove Plaza. Owner David Taylor has created a miniworld of the French provinces, with 10 tables dressed in provençal patterns, fresh flowers, soft taped French music, and first-rate dishes. Start with an escargot, coquille, or *crepes farcis* (stuffed crepe), then move on to a *queue de homard provencale* (lobster tail) or boeuf stroganoff flambe, or any of the ever-changing eight entrees. Open for lunch and dinner (11 A.M. to about 10 P.M.); not inexpensive (over $25 per person) and worth it! Also noted for an exceptional wine cellar.

Eva (of Venice) has opened **Evita's** (974–2333), "the best little pasta house in Jamaica," high on a hill at Mantalent Inn (also reachable from MoBay), that's become an instant hit with visitors. Both pasta and prices are desirable: *rotelle alla Eva* (under $10), *escargot casalinga* (about $10), lobster fettuccine, lasagna "Rastafari" (only fresh vegetables), chef Pablo's own oyster mushroom sauce. There are meat dishes as well, and sinful desserts. Reservations needed or plan a people-watching sit-in at the bar in this almost 100-year-old colonial house.

A favorite is the **Jungle Hut** (no phone) on the White River (under the bridge), a haunt for the rich and famous and local Rastas. It features dirt floors; wood benches; slapboard tables; huge, haunting murals of Bob Marley, Haile Selassie, Marcus Garvey, and Paul Bogle; and the muted sounds of the rushing White River. The good news: fried chicken and grilled lobster. The bad news: Prices are escalating due to international underground popularity. The lobster, for instance, costs $100.

A short walk further on Main, near the roundabout and clock tower, the **Parkway** (974–2667) is short on atmosphere but long on good Jamaican fare, steaks, and lobster at prices that start at only $7. That's why it's crowded with local clientele. Come as you are from 7:30 A.M. to 11:30 P.M.

If you walk south from the roundabout (away from the sea) and right on DaCosta Drive, you'll spot **The Ruins** (974–2442). Lovely public gardens cover the hillside, a 40-foot-high waterfall cascades into the Turtle River, and you cross into the dining area over a footbridge. The menu is extensive, but regulars know the Chinese cuisine is best and the really best advice may be to sip, not stay to sup.

About four miles east of the town center along coastal Route A1, **Casanova** (974–2353) in the Sans Souci Hotel is a magical place. Stylish, romantic, with views of the hotel's gardens, Casanova also boasts superb service and perhaps the most ambitious kitchen in the area. Specialties include flambéed dishes: supreme of chicken, steak au poivre vert, chicken and lobster panache, plus homemade pasta and other Italian renditions. Figure about $35 per person without drinks or wine. Dress up a little (jackets not required), and make reservations. Open for lunch and dinner daily; closed in summer.

About half a mile further east, the **Kings Arms** (974–4233), on the open-air patio of Harmony Hall great house, is good for everything from steak-and-kidney pie or fish and chips to lobster. Best of all, you can eat well for under $5. Open daily for lunch, snacks, and dinner.

PORT ANTONIO

The **Bonnie View Hotel** (993–2752) on Bonnie View Road above town has lovely views of the twin harbors, a pleasant afternoon tea, plus home-style dinners—Cajun chicken, blackened redfish, roast pork chasseur, even a vegetarian platter—at budget prices. Expect to be satisfied for $10 or more per person. Open daily for breakfast, lunch, and dinner. On the peninsula between the harbors, the gingerbread-like **DeMontevin Lodge** (993–2604), on Musgrave and George streets, is a family-run place that will treat you like one of their own at dinnertime if you call a day ahead for reservations. The owner used to cook for Errol Flynn. About $15 or so per person.

Flynn himself hung out on **Navy Island,** a 64-acre island reachable by five-minute ferry from Port Antonio for about $3. Present owners Alice and Harry Eiler of New York welcome visitors and yachts to the Admiralty Club for lunch or dinner (only with advance reservations: 993–2667). A five-course dinner, featuring an entree of lobster, chicken Kiev, braised pork chops, or chicken en vin, runs about $28 per person. Seafood is served the day it's caught, and local specialties—pepperpot soup, ackee and saltfish, calaloo soup—turn up regularly. Classical music tapes are played in the evening, and on Saturday nights there's barefoot disco dancing to live music.

A serious, if simple, favorite is **Mr. Simpson's Restaurant** (no phone), 1 Upper Williams Street, which is open 24 hours a day. There are only five tiny tables tucked into this equally tiny and clean restaurant on the edge of the food and crafts market. You'll hear it before you see it, because the boombox from LimeLight Records is next door, but it's a fascinating people-watching spot. The Simpson family cook and serve fried chicken, curried goat, Creole snapper or jack, and stewed peas and rice, all at minimal prices (around $5).

Splendid and special, **Trident Villas and Hotel** (993–2602) offers one of the best dining experiences in Jamaica, if not in the Caribbean. The sterling gleams and the cut crystal shines in this intimate, elegant room as your seven-course meal, served by white-gloved waiters, begins. The menu changes daily—there is no choice of selections—but put yourself in the hands of Trident's capable chef. A sample meal: hearts of palm, red-pea soup, steamed lobster in tarragon butter, avocado vinaigrette, tournedos of beef with potato and callaloo, champagne sherbet, coffee with Tia Maria.

This prix-fixe feast costs about $40 per person, not including wine. Open daily for dinner; reservations should be made by 5 P.M. Jacket and tie are required for men in winter season, jacket only at other times.

A short distance east of Trident is the much more modest **Castle Cove** (no phone). It's a thatched-roof affair near water's edge with a friendly atmosphere. The food they serve is delicious and extremely reasonably priced. Steamed butterfish with ample amounts of well-seasoned rice and peas, plus yams, goes for under $5. No credit cards.

Boston Bay, just beyond, is *the* place for jerk pork. Jerk chicken and jerk fish are fine, too. Pick out a beachside vendor and join the legion of "jerk lovers."

KINGSTON

As you would expect of Jamaica's capital and largest metropolitan area, Kingston offers the island's most varied restaurant scene, including such ethnic fare as Chinese, Indian, German, Korean, Mexican, and Middle Eastern.

Probably the most famous—and certainly the most romantic—dining spot locally is a half-hour drive out of town. The **Blue Mountain Inn** (927–1700) on the Gordon Town Road (Route B1), a great house built in 1754 on a coffee plantation, sits on the banks of the Hope River in the mountains, surrounded by dense vegetation. Cocktails are served out on the terrace, and dinner follows in the elegant, candle-lit dining room inside.

The menu is Continental with the occasional Jamaican accent, as in the ackee quiche. Pork prepared with cognac and sour cream, as well as scallops of lobster sauteed with shallots, are prized by many, although it is only fair to say that the magnificent surroundings overshadow the kitchen on some nights. The wine list is superior, perhaps the best on the island, with imported vintages starting at about $15. Expect to pay about $30 per person for dinner, not including drinks or wine.

Jackets are required for gentlemen, and ladies should be prepared for the cool of the mountain night on the terrace. The Blue Mountain is open for dinner only, from 7:30 to 9:30 P.M., except Sunday. Reservations are a must.

If you don't have a rental car, a limousine service operates from the Courtleigh, Oceana, Jamaica Pegasus, and Terra Nova hotels; the round trip is about $5. Otherwise, taxi fare there and back will cost around twice that.

A garden restaurant at 8 Belmont Road, **Norma's** (929 –4966) has been an *in* spot since the owner opened her nonexistent doors in 1985. Since then, it's become not only a lunchtime favorite with the present Prime Minister's wife and the ladies-who-lunch, but also with Kingston movers-and-shakers. The waiters serve picture-perfect dishes that are all elegantly arranged according to color, design, and texture and accompanied by flower blossoms. And the dishes are devine: fillet of fish grilled in a caper sauce, grilled devil crab back, spicy chicken in parsley rice, chicken breast stuffed with cream cheese, a Greek salad. The herbs and spices used are grown in the surrounding gardens. The desserts are appropriately caloric: chocolate double jeopardy, soursop mousse, piña colada mousse. Owner Norma Shirley has designed food pages for *Vogue* Magazine and is in the process of opening another Norma-at-the-Renaissance on Glouster Avenue in Montego Bay. A very upscale place at upscale prices, with dinner starting at $40.

Minnie, a former cook for Bob Marley, now owns her own **Minnie's Ethiopean Herbal Health Food Restaurant** (927–9207), at 176 Hope Road. True to the Rasta code, she serves no meat or dishes with salt, but she does serve spicy fish balls, red-pea stew, broad-bean stew, brown-stew fish, callaloo and akee, and vegetable run-dun. Dishes start at $10. She prepares fresh herbal teas and juices unlimited (soursop, carrot, beet root, papaya, June plum, orange sorrell, neaseberry, Otaheite apple, mango, tamarind, cucumber) for about $1. The best time to visit is Friday night (about 8 to 10), when musicians introduce reggae vibes in the upstairs gallery. Come early and stay late for a Jamaican breakfast of "callaloo with food" (yams, pumpkin, banana, and rice) or ackee with festival (fried dumplings) for about $3.

In the New Kingston area, the **Surrey Tavern** (926–3690) in the Jamaica Pegasus Hotel is an English-style pub that features a popular, reasonably priced luncheon buffet. On Friday and Saturday evenings (from 7:30 to 9:30 P.M.), sample the steak-and-kidney pie or other pub fare while listening to good live jazz. Lunch is served weekdays only.

Seventeen floors up, the elegant **Talk of the Town** (926–3690) offers both spectacular city views and a menu that is elaborate. Candlelight dining is special, with an ever-changing menu. Open for lunch weekdays, dinner daily from 7 P.M.; reservations and jackets for men are suggested.

Nearby, in the Wyndham New Kingston, the panoramic rooftop vistas are stunning, the ambience is upscale, and the fare is simply delicious at the rooftop restaurant on the 17th floor. Musicians contribute to the ambience in the evenings. Plan on $25 or more per person, sans liquor. Open for lunch weekdays; dinner served daily. Jackets are required for men, and reservations are a good idea.

At Hope and Waterloo roads, **The Grog Shop** (926–3580) is on the back patio of the government-owned Devon House, facing a serene courtyard edged by attractive shops. The staff dresses in 19th-century garb, the traditional Jamaican cuisine is well prepared, and it's hard to imagine a more pleasing setting to shut out the big city beyond. You can grab a quick snack here, such as a crab cake (about $2), or head for the new "Devonshire," within the same complex, with more elaborate settings and cuisine. Before or after, stroll across the way and try a scoop of soursop ice cream (about 50 cents) at **I Scream** or a plantain tart (40 cents) at **The Bread Basket.** Open for lunch and dinner daily, except Sunday; reservations advisable for dinner.

The **Terra Nova** (926–2211), 17 Waterloo Road, is a former private residence turned hotel and restaurant that attracts Kingston society and government types. The menu is Continental, and you can expect to pay $20 or more apiece at dinner. The fun here is the crowd, and the late-evening scene—the place is a hot dance spot and nightclub, as well. Open for breakfast, lunch, and dinner daily. Reservations are a good idea for dinner, and so are jackets for gentlemen.

Another hotel that draws crowds for its food is the hospitable **Mayfair** (926–1610), 4 West King's House Close, near the parklike grounds that surround the government buildings, King's House, and Jamaica House. Jim and Sybil Hughes are genial hosts of the popular poolside buffet (about $10 on Wednesday evenings) and Saturday night barbecues ($7 to $10) from 7:30 to 9 P.M. Reservations are strongly suggested.

In Port Royal across Kingston harbor, **Morgan's Harbour** (924–8464) serves breakfast, lunch, and dinner. You can't beat the view—yachts bobbing in the marina only feet from your table, the harbor and skyline of Kingston beyond. You can't beat the relaxed, get-away-from-it-all ambience either—elegantly casual. And the kitchen? Make straight for the fresh seafood, with lobster cocktail at about $2, and a whole grilled lobster for about $15. Open daily, except Sunday.

MANDEVILLE

Hotel Astra (962–3265), 62 Ward Avenue, serves breakfast, lunch, and dinner daily in a pleasant, informal setting. Nicely prepared international and Jamaican entrees, including lobster thermidor and fresh-fish specials, range from about $6.50 to $15. The Friday-night poolside barbecue is popular, as is the Sunday breakfast buffet. The hotel's **Revival Room Pub** also offers homemade pizza, burgers, and seafood salads.

A long-standing Mandeville favorite has been **Bill Laurie's Steak House** (962–3116) in Bloomfield Gardens. Set

on a hilltop with spectacular views of the town and surrounding countryside, the restaurant is a 150-year-old hotel
known for steaks, chops, and fresh fish, all cooked to order.
With Bill Laurie's recent death, his cook, Enid, is continuing
the Laurie tradition, and nothing can change the ambience
—a collection of antique cars, license plates from around
the world, and yellowing business cards. Figure on about
$15 per person, without drinks. Open daily for lunch and
dinner, except Sunday. No credit cards.

Nightlife

Jamaica's biggest spectacle is absolutely free and occurs nightly. Sunset, it's called. At places like Rick's Cafe in Negril, high on a cliff at the island's westernmost vantage point, the setting of Old Sol each day is a celebration marked by ahs of appreciation, rum drinks raised in toast, and the emergence of that good-times-seeking creature, the nocturnal party animal. He or she has come to the right island, for making merry into the wee hours is standard operating procedure in the major resort areas. And wherever you are, it all begins with a few moments' pause to bid farewell to the heat of day. And to welcome the night—be it cultured or crazy, cool or red hot.

Prices quoted for the following nightspots and events are in U.S. currency.

BARS, CABARETS, AND CLUBS

The island's bars, clubs, and cabarets give you the choice of soft, romantic background music, reverberating disco tunes, hypnotic reggae, or many steps in between.

Keep this in mind: Wherever there's a large resort hotel, you'll find a smorgasbord of nightlife—and lots of fellow lovers of the night—under one roof. The competition for your business is such that each hotel manager is constantly on the lookout for ways to get you happily through the night. This is especially so when the hotel is situated on the outskirts, beyond easy walking distance to anywhere else.

If you're in Montego Bay or Ocho Rios, the two most developed tourist havens, finding nighttime fun is as easy as strolling through the center of things and keeping an eye peeled and an ear cocked. If one place isn't quite your style, proceed to the next. In sprawling, confusing Kingston and in less raucous towns like Port Antonio, Mandeville, and Negril, some advance planning is required to keep your scouting time to a minimum.

Of course, of all there is to see and do in Jamaica, the night scene is the most changeable. Clubs come and go; the hot spot now is replaced by another in a few months' time. Here's our list of favorites . . .

NEGRIL

In Negril, when the sun goes down, the music men come out. The insider's favorite place remains **Kaiser's Cafe** (957–4450), at the West End. If there are any really hot reggae stars in town, chances are, they're here. Greg Isaacs, Dennis Brown, and Freddie McGregor all perform from time to time, along with lesser knowns. Depending on performers, admission ranges from $4 to $10, and Wednesday and Friday are action nights, starting at 9:30.

De Buss (957–4405), on Norman Manley Boulevard, also has its set of permanent fans. The bus, which stands at the entrance gate, was the one used in the movie *Live and Let Die,* and while it's the worse-for-James-Bond-wear, the double-decker is easily spotted. Owner Joy Logan feels she has the best shows on Tuesday and Sunday nights, when reggae bands arrive around 10 and special artists show up around midnight. Eddie FitzRoy, the Fabulous Five, and Greg Isaacs have recently made the scene, at admission charges that range from $4 to $7. At press time, Saturday night buffet was slated with dancing on the beach that fronts the raised bandstand.

Rick's Cafe (957–4335), on the lighthouse road south of town, remains famous for sunset-watching. Live jam sessions until 11 are occasionally featured.

Another possibility for reggae is the **Negril Tree House Club** (957–4287) on Norman Manley Boulevard along the beach. Monday is floor show and barbecue night, with free transportation for those who need it.

Gotta dance? Do it to both reggae and stateside sounds at one of the liveliest discos on the island—at **Hedonism II** (957–4200), Rutland Point, on the seven-mile beach. Opens at 11 P.M. nightly. A $40 package includes a meal and all drinks.

A sister resort, the luxe **Grand Lido** (957–4010), nestled next door in beachfront splendor, has a special night pass for outside guests for dinner at Negril's finest restaurant, the Cafe Lido, followed by unlimited drinks, live entertainment, a swinging disco, and midnight buffet. Cost is about $80, at this most upscale place, and the Friday gala buffet night is particularly trendy. Reservations necessary.

Last, but hardly least, hit the **Compulseion Disco** (957–4416), at Shop 24, Plaza de Negril. If their band has closed up shop, it's time you did, too!

MONTEGO BAY

No doubt about it, Montego Bay is the party capital of Jamaica. The highlights: On the downtown beachfront hotel strip, the action is at **Fantasy Disco** in the Casa Montego Hotel (952–4150), 2 Kent Avenue. It's open from 10 P.M. to 3 A.M. nightly, and a cover charge of $17 includes drinks. For a more subdued evening, try the nightly piano bar at **Doctor's Cave Beach Hotel** (952–4355) on Gloucester Avenue near the famous white sand of the same name.

The really happening place is **Pier 1-On-The-Waterfront** (952–2452), on Howard Cooke Boulevard, that sets the pace on Friday nights with their happy hour and a dusk-to-dawn disco.

On Sunset Drive at the south end of the bay, off the picturesque inlet known as Montego Bay Freeport, the **Cave** disco is a solid hit at the Seawind Beach Resort (952–4874). The club opens at 10 P.M. nightly, and admission is $5.

On the coast Route A1 in the Rose Hall area, the club called **Witch's Hideaway** at Rose Hall Holiday Inn (953–2485) has withstood the test of time. It gets going at 10 P.M. every night, and there is a $5 cover charge.

OCHO RIOS

The Ruins (974–2442) on DaCosta Drive just south of the Ocho Rios roundabout is the town's foremost venue for meeting and greeting. With its spectacular mountain waterfall and lily ponds, the surroundings themselves are enough —but the bar serves an honest drink, too. The bar stays open until 10:30 P.M., and a steel band plays for most of the night. This scenic spot is frequented mostly by touring visitors and cruise ship passengers.

The **Little Pub** (974–2324) in the heart of town has a nightly 10 P.M. show featuring calypso and dance music. Admission is $10. The disco action is best at **Silks** at the Shaw Park Beach (974–2552) on the coast Route A3 shortly before the White River bridge. It opens at 9 P.M. nightly; cover charge is $5. Another hot spot is **Maroons** at the Americana Hotel (974–2151) on Mallard's Beach, which opens at 10 P.M. nightly with a $3 admission.

Savvy visitors will make their way to the **Acropolis Disco** (974–2633) on Main Street, opposite the Silver Seas Hotel, to dance until dawn with smooth-steppin' locals. Admission: about $5.

PORT ANTONIO

In Port Antonio, **Fern Hill** (993–3222) is on a local hill of the same name and keeps the neighborhood lively with a live reggae show at 9:30 P.M. on Friday nights. About $30 covers the cost of dinner, the show, and drinks. If you want to rub shoulders with the *real* Jamaica, go directly to the **Roof Club,** 11 West Street. The entrance fee is about $1, and from about 11 on, this is the only place to be. Friday and Saturday nights are dynamite, whether the music is live or taped. There are a couple of other clubs **(Blue Jays, Centre Point),** but the Roof Club remains top of the disco list. None have telephones.

KINGSTON

In Kingston, the Jamaica Pegasus Hotel (926–3690) at 81 Knutsford Boulevard houses two admirable nightspots. The **Surrey Tavern,** a friendly English-style pub by day, turns into the hottest place to hear live jazz on Thursday nights. The sounds start around 7 P.M. Up on the 17th floor, at **Talk of the Town,** there's always the spectacular view of the city and often a good combo or singer after 8 P.M.

At the nearby Wyndham Kingston (926–5430), 77 Knutsford Boulevard, the **Jonkanoo Lounge** features slick nightclub-type acts with an 11 P.M. showtime and a cover charge of about $5.

One of the newest discos is **Illusions** (929–2125), on South Avenue at the Lane Shopping Plaza. On weekends, this is where sharp locals come to dance.

The **Atlantis Night Club** (929–4387), 69 Knutsford Boulevard, describes itself as "the Jamaican way to play." This disco opens at 11 P.M. Thursday through Saturday; admission is $7. Another local favorite in the New Kingston area on Thursday through Saturday is the **Epiphany** disco (929–1130), 1 St. Lucia Avenue. Cover charge is $10.

The **Terra Nova Hotel** (926–2211), 17 Waterloo Road,

is the place where you may see a government minister dancing with, presumably, his wife. This former private residence is a hangout for Kingston society and high bureaucrats. The fun begins after 9 P.M. **Mingles,** the nightspot at the Courtleigh Hotel (926–8174), 31 Trafalgar Road, is a hit with both visiting and resident Brits. Open nightly; admission is $8.

MANDEVILLE

In little-known Mandeville is lesser-known **1907 Gallery** (962–0109), at 1907 Caledonia Meadows (*see* Exploring section of "The Inland Island" chapter). You'll need a local to get you there. Open nightly until 10; the drinks are good and the conversation is the best.

Bill Laurie's Steak House (962–3116) in Mandeville's Bloomfield Gardens is just the place to while away a more sedate evening. This hilltop aerie affords great views, and the bar couldn't be cozier or more atmospheric with its dark wood, antique auto license plates, and yellowed business cards from former patrons tacked to every available space. The grand piano sits nearby, and no one will laugh if you sit down to play. Open daily.

The **Revival Room Pub** in the Hotel Astra (962–3265), 62 Ward Avenue, is another convivial spot frequented by both locals and visitors to this tidy, alpine-like city. The Mandeville visitor information center is located at the hotel, and so this is a good place to begin any tour of the environs, day or night. The center is open 24 hours. The pub is open daily.

To check out the local disco scene—remember, this is not really a tourist town—ask for directions to **Planet** or **Tracks,** both in Mandeville Plaza; **Intime** in Willogate Shopping Center; or **Zee-X** in Caledonia Plaza. None has a phone, and not all may be open nightly.

BOONOONOONOOS

In local patois, the word means as good as it gets, something extraordinary. At all the larger resort hotels, there's at least one *boonoonoonoos* event weekly, usually a torchlit-poolside or beachfront buffet or barbecue, accompanied by strolling calypso musicians or a steel band and then capped off with a show—double-jointed limbo dancers, barefooted walkers on live coals, and the like. It's all worth seeing, at least once.

But the *boonoonoonoos* have only just begun. Tuesday through Thursday during the winter season, your **Evening on the Great River** starts with pick up at your hotel and a drive to the Montego River west of town; there you paddle upstream by torchlight in a dugout canoe, then hike a short distance to the "jungle clearing" where a recreated Awarak Indian village, drinks, dinner, and festive entertainment awaits. It all costs about $38 per person; make reservations through your hotel or call Great River Productions Ltd. (952–5047).

In Ocho Rios the same kind of fun happens on Sundays and Tuesdays, and is called **Jamaica Night on the White River.** In this case, the evening includes round-trip transportation from your hotel, a canoe ride up river, open bar, reggae-and-rock floor show, and dancing under the stars. Remember to take mosquito repellent. Tickets cost about $30 for adults, $20 for children and should be purchased at your hotel activities desk.

THEATER, DANCE, AND CLASSICAL MUSIC

Jamaicans have an abiding fondness for the performing arts, and you can enjoy them, too, in the country's cultural center, Kingston. From late December through early spring, the **National Pantomime** performs its yearly update of *Trash* (from the local phrase "trash and ready," meaning "good"), a folk musical with original songs and dances, bright sets and costumes, and amusing commentary on current affairs, at the Ward Theater on North Parade. For information call 922–7071.

The concert season of the **Jamaica School of Dance** runs from late January to early February. Its interpretative dance based on Caribbean movements and themes is performed at the Little Theatre (926–6603), 4 Tom Redgam Avenue. The internationally known **National Dance Theatre Company** performs at the Little Theatre for a few days in early December and then again from mid-July to mid-August. The NDTC Singers are also part of this group.

For classical music, check with your hotel activities desk or *The Daily Gleaner* for performances by the **Institute of Jamaica's School of Music,** the **Jamaica Philharmonic Symphony Orchestra,** and the **National Chorale.** Most concerts are in the early winter and early summer months.

SUNSETS BY WATER

If sunset-watching by land is *irie* ("excellent"), sunset-watching by sea is the *irie*-est. Strike up a friendship with a local yachtsman if you can. Failing that, there are a few seagoing outfits that will not only sail you into the sunset but ply you with grog and/or grub as well. These cruises last about two hours and cost $25 to $60.

In Montego Bay, two vessels that offer sunset cruises dock at On the Waterfront on Howard Cook Highway, opposite the Montego Bay Craft Market. You can be picked up at your hotel for either cruise. The **Calico** (952–5860), a 55-foot ketch, is an old wooden sailer kept in impeccable condition; it was used in the Walt Disney production, *Return to Treasure Island.* The **Topaz** (952–2955) is a 115-foot, square-rigged schooner.

From Port Antonio, the catamaran **Lady Jamaica** (no phone) makes a daily cocktail sail. Make arrangements through your hotel to climb aboard.

Shopping

Jamaica proves the adage that shoppers are made, not born. Not only is the potential for purchasing virtually limitless—from duty-free goods at substantial savings to island-made fashions, barely basic bikinis, serious artwork, wood carvings, silk batik, and hand-rolled cigars with personally embossed bands.

Native entrepreneurs—known as higglers hereabouts—will approach you frequently and with varying degrees of persistence; they'll be trying to sell you everything from the illegal *ganja*—marijuana—to "gold" jewelry to a combination coin bank and ashtray fashioned from a length of bamboo. If you're not interested—and in the case of ganja, or any other illicit drug, to make a purchase is to risk arrest—say so firmly but politely; that will almost always suffice. If you are interested, it's negotiation time.

A rule of thumb about bargaining: If the item is marked with a price, chances are it is nonnegotiable.

DUTY-FREE SHOPPING

You *may* save as much as 40 to 50 percent off U.S. prices. Then, again, you may save much less. A little pre-planning makes all the difference. Before you leave home, decide what "in-bond" items you're interested in—be they a Swiss timepiece, French perfume, British woolens, Irish crystal, camera or recording gear, gold jewelry, European crystal, porcelain, bone china, liquor (including such Jamaican products as rums, the coffee liqueur Tia Maria, or rum liqueur Rumona), tobacco products (Royal Jamaica cigars are prized), or Jamaican-made fragrances like Khus Khus perfume or Royall Lyme, Royall Spice, or Royall Bay after-shave for men. Check U.S. prices. Then there will be no doubt.

Keep in mind, too, that you may still have to pay U.S. Customs duty on any purchases that exceed the $400 limit per adult, which includes one liter of liquor.

Shopping duty-free goes like this: You must have I.D. and pay with U.S. or Canadian currency, traveler's check, or credit card. Liquor and tobacco products can only be purchased at the airport or pier. Most in-bond shops are grouped in shopping centers, in major hotels, or at the airports. While the shops may have exclusive brands or patterns, prices for types of merchandise are about the same no matter where you go. Hours are standard, too—from 8:30 or 9 A.M. to 5 P.M. on weekdays, till 6 P.M. on Saturdays.

MADE IN JAMAICA

Jamaica is a country of crafts. Almost everyone, it sometimes seems, is a fashioner of straw, wood, fabric, beads, or gemstones. You can encounter amazing and unexpected craftsmanship anywhere—at a rickety roadside stand, from a grinning local man who approaches you on a street corner to a small boy who is an obvious expert at catching your eye and making his sales pitch.

Among the things Jamaicans do best: carvings, bowls, boxes, and other items made of lignum vitae, a rosy hardwood; woven straw baskets and mats; wicker furniture and other goods; beautiful hand-embroidered linens; cotton and silk batiked in stunning colors; stylish, silk-screened fashions; and jewelry made from black coral, coral agate, or shells. Jamaican art is prized by international collectors.

Quality varies widely, and, as you might expect, most of the very best ends up in the tourist boutiques and shops at prices to match. Our shopping strategy: If you find the *very* Jamaican-made thing you want, buy it then and there. Except for the most ordinary straw goods, it's not likely that you'll find that exact item elsewhere. (This is a land of individual artisans, not standardized tourist gimcracks.) But if you aren't quite sure, or think the price is too high, look for a reasonable facsimile—at a cheaper price—at one of the government-sponsored craft markets.

NEGRIL

Negril isn't known for shopping, but the **Negril Craft Park,** which at first glimpse looks like every other hohum muster of 120-plus shopping stalls, turns out to be terrific. This is the place to find what may be the Caribbean's finest T-shirt—a replica of Mickey Mouse with his hair in dreadlocks and the phrase, "Mickey Gone Dread." It's also the place to to check out Sammy of "Sammy's wood carvings," and his hand-crafted pieces, or Minnie and her coral jewelry pieces.

Several minishops at the **Plaza de Negril** offer a small selection of perfume, imported leathers, and so forth. **Gail's Place** (no phone), at 3 Adrija Plaza, has bathings suits for him and her, film, and suntan lotion. If you can't leave without a super-sexy poster, the **Omni Duty Free Shop** (957–4312), also on Adrija Plaza, has some of the best. Later this year, a new shopping plaza opens its gates at West End, next to King's Plaza.

MONTEGO BAY

Some of the finest finds in Jamaica nestle within the crowded confines of **Liz DeLisser's Gallery of West Indian Art** (952–4547) at 1 Orange Lane. The gallery, which offers some of the most interesting Jamaican and Haitian paintings found anywhere at a good range in prices, also has wonderful wooden fantasy animals, birds, and fish. These wonderful creatures range from $10 to $40. Mrs. DeLisser also has another treasure trove at nearby Round Hill (952–5150).

This is the land of reggae, so it's also the place to pick up tapes and records. Check out **Record City** (993–2836), Westgate Plaza, MoBay; and **Jimmy Cliff's Records** (no phone) at Oneness Square.

Another favorite is **Sprigs and Things** (952–4735), on St. James Place, Gloucester Avenue, where artist Janie Soren paints whimsical animals, birds, and flowers on tennis togs, fabric totes, and sarongs.

At the airport, the **Montego Bay Duty Free Shop** (952–2377) handles electronic equipment and cameras by the likes of Nikon, Panasonic, and Vivitar. It's run by the same folks who have the **Chulani Camera Centre** (952–2158) in the City Centre Building near Sam Sharpe Square.

The **City Centre Building,** in fact, as well as the **Casa Montego Arcade** at the Casa Montego Hotel opposite Cornwall Beach, have a cluster of duty-free shops. At the former, look for the **Presita Shop** (952–3261) for stereo and camera buys. At the latter, the MoBay branch of **Swiss Stores** (952–3087) carries an excellent selection of name-brand watches, electronic gear, and jewelry.

In the Rose Hall area, another **Swiss Stores** (953–2520) is at the Half Moon Club, as is the **Holiday Duty Free Shop** (953–2053), which specializes in photographic equipment. The Holiday Inn also houses a **Holiday Duty Free** (953–2503). Another mecca of duty-free shopping can be found at the **Holiday Village Shopping Centre** across Route A1 from the Holiday Inn.

For island-made crafts and foodstuffs, **Things Jamai-**

can Ltd. (952–1936) at the airport has a small but interesting array. In the Montego Bay Freeport area, the **Tree
Trunk Shop** (952–4911) has splendid offerings in Jamaican
hardwood furnishings and wicker.

Along Harbour Street, near the wharves where fishermen unload their daily catch, is the **Crafts Market**. Bargain for the best deal on straw hats, baskets, mats,
and other island products. For higher quality wood carvings
and hand-turned bowls, look up the **Native Shop** (952–
2992) at the Beachview Shopping Plaza on Gloucester Avenue.

For island fashions for women, **Ruth Clarage** has
branches in Freeport (952–3278), in the Casa Montego
Hotel (952–2282), and at Holiday Village (953–2579)
across from the Holiday Inn in the Rose Hall area. Other
fashionable options: the **Pineapple Shops** at Freeport
(952–0652) and the Montego Beach Hotel (952–5003) on
Gloucester Avenue.

FALMOUTH

At the Trelawny Beach Hotel east of town, this branch
of **Chulani** specializes in savings on crystal (Waterford,
Orrefors, and others), figurines (Hummel), and perfume.

Caribatik (954–3314), on the coast Route A1 two miles
east of Falmouth, is worth a stop whether you're in the
buying mood or not. This is the studio, shop, and gallery
of Chicago-native Muriel Chandler, an engaging artist who
has taken the vibrant colors of Jamaica and the surrounding
sea, and rendered them spectacularly onto baticked cotton
and silk. Both French and American designers have used
her silks. As you would expect, you'll find batik shirts, ties,
dresses, and caftans here, but you can also buy her fabric by
the yard. Best of all, ask to see her gallery of batik "paintings"—many of which hang in homes, institutions, and col-
lections the world over. Open mid-November to mid-May
from 10 A.M. to 3 P.M., Tuesday through Saturday.

OCHO RIOS

There are four shopping centers in Ocho Rios. The newest, **Island Plaza,** houses an outstanding collection of worthwhile shops. Start at **Caktus** (974–5423), very upscale, with designer duds, French perfumes, and jewelry. **Jack-in-the-Box** (no phone) is nestled almost next door, with Jamaican coffees, cigars, and liqueurs, all packaged for customs approval. Here they also offer a free taste of the different coffees, from almost impossible to find Blue Mountain coffee to mixtures of High Mountain coffee. **Coconut Joe** (952–7823) has one of the best Bob Marley T-shirts anywhere, a haunting study of Marley's face. The **Frame Centre Gallery** (974–2374), a branch of its Kingston big brother, has fine art and wood sculptures at serious art prices.

Then, move on to **Ocean Village,** the country's largest shopping plaza, is at seaside next to Turtle Beach Towers. **Swiss Stores** (974–2519) displays its Swiss watches, electronic equipment, and handcrafted jewelry there. **Soni's** (974–2303) has fine linens, French perfumes, gold chains, and ivory jewelry.

Pineapple Place is on the shoreside of Main Street in the heart of town. An impressive array of Japanese and German cameras and accessories are for sale at the **Caribbean Camera Centre** (974–2421). **Casa De'Oro** (974–2577) has jewelry, watches (Cartier, Corum, Gucci, Movado, Seiko, Swatch), and perfumes. A short walk east, on the inland side of the street opposite the Plantation Inn, is **Coconut Grove Shopping Centre.** Here, the many duty-free emporiums include **Americana Freeport Shop** (974–2414), which carries French perfumes, gold jewelry, linens, crystal (Waterford, Lalique, Swarovski), and china (Wedgwood, Royal Doulton).

For Jamaican-made gift items, sample **Living Wood** (974–2601), **The Craft Cottage** (974–2249), or **Under the Rainbow** (974–5158) in the Ocean Village Shopping Centre.

Plan a stop at the Sans Souci Hotel, Club and Spa, to

visit their boutique at the gatehouse. Here, Busha Browne marmalades, pepper jellies, spicy chutneys, spicy piquant sauces, and pepper sherry are for sale. They also offer wonderful wood fantasy animals, along with Kingston-made Ital-Craft belts and paperback books.

Ruth Clarage has exclusive designs for both day and evening wear for women. Look for them at her stores in Pineapple Place (974–2658) and Ocean Village (974–2874).

East of Ocho Rios on the coast road, **Harmony Hall** (974–4222) is a restored 19th-century great house devoted to the best in Jamaican contemporary art and artisans. One example among many: the distinctive and sought-after wood Annabella Boxes, named for their originator, Annabella Proudlock, a Harmony Hall director. They come in all sizes and feature Jamaican art on their covers. Harmony Hall also has original canvases, maps, charts, and crafts, and changing art exhibits and Sunday openings.

PORT ANTONIO

The finds here are unique. The downtown **Crafts Market** is crowded and creative. This is the place to fill your picnic basket with local fruits and to find wonderful carved birds. Charlie Brown in stall #35 has wonderful creations in ebony, lignum vitae, and mahogany. This is also the place to find good, inexpensive Jamaican sandals, unlimited bottled spices, or a Rasta knit hat.

Sang Hing Giftland (993–2716) in the City Centre Plaza in the heart of town is the place to go for duty-free items. It stocks a treasure trove of imported bone china, crystal, figurines, jewelry, and more.

A more tranquil venue at which to pursue native hardwood furnishing and wicker is the shop aptly named **Oasis** (993–3745), 1 Harbour Street.

The widow of Hollywood legend Errol Flynn, Patricia Wymore Flynn, owns the small **Designer's Gallery,** in the Jamaica Palace Hotel (993–3294), which is open Tuesday through Sunday, 10 A.M. to 6 P.M. Mrs. Flynn uses pizzaz and patience to gather her collection of belts, painted cotton shirts, colorful shorts for men, and sweeping silks for ladies. A branch of the menswear retailer, **Farel Ltd.** (993–3311), is located at the City Centre Plaza.

KINGSTON

At the airport, you'll find branches of **Motta and Swiss Stores** (924–8023), which stock renowned watches (Juvenia, Omega, Patek Philippe, Piaget, Rolex, etc.) and electronic gear (Sony, Panasonic, and many more), as well as one-of-a-kind jewelry. Other outlets are at the Jamaica Pegasus Hotel (929–8147) in New Kingston; 107 Harbour Street (922–8050); and the Constant Spring Mall (926–4861), 20 Constant Spring Road.

For Jamaican items you'll do no better than the shops behind Devon House that comprise **Things Jamaican Ltd.** (929–6602), 26 Hope Road. From a lignum-vitae coaster at under $1 to handmade four-poster beds at several hundred, this is a collection of the best craftsmanship on the island in a highly browsable, no-pressure setting. There's also a small shop at the airport (924–8556).

Near the cruise piers on the harbor, the **Jamaica Crafts Market** (922–3015), 52 Port Royal Street, houses a vast assortment of handmade items, with a special bounty of straw and woven goods and wood carvings. Hours are 8 A.M. to 5 P.M. Monday to Friday; open till 6 P.M. Saturdays.

Kingston has a number of shopping centers and plazas. Two of the newest and best are **The Springs** on Half Way Tree Road, with one of the best bookstores on the island, simply called The Bookstore, and serious designer boutiques; and the **New Kingston Shopping Centre** on Dominica Drive across from the Tourism Centre Building. On two levels, with an open-air central court that has a gurgling fountain and reflecting pool, there are more than three dozen shops, as well as free underground parking and a food court. Check out the gleaming hardwood furnishings at **Skandia** (929–8630), the stylish sportswear and swimwear at **Just Wright** (929–8612), and the fashions for women at **California by Philip** (929–4373).

Nearby, at the Wyndham Kingston Hotel (926–5430) is a small but select art gallery; the Jamaica Pegasus Hotel next door at 81 Knutsford Boulevard has their own underground gallery. Both are worth a visit, but both have higher prices than the smaller galleries now proliferating in Kingston. The **Frame Centre Gallery** (926–4644) at 10 Tangerine Place, is one of the originators, as are the **Upstairs-Downstairs Gallery** (922–8260) on Harbour Street, the **Gallery Makonde** (926–5776) on Waterloo Avenue, the **Contemporary Art Centre** (927–9958), 1 Liguanea Avenue, and the **Bolivar Bookshop and Gallery** (926–8799) at Grove and Half Way Tree roads.

MANDEVILLE

Mandeville has four shopping plazas. **Willogate Shopping Centre** is at Wesley and Manchester roads. **Grove Court Shopping Centre** is just off the town square. **Caledonia Shopping Centre** is on Caledonia Road near South Race Course.

Manchester Shopping Centre is also on Caledonia Road, near Newgreen Road. For island-made souvenirs here, check out **Craft Things Jamaican** (962–3363).

The **SWA Craft Centre** (962–0694) at 42 Hargreaves Avenue makes its own version of Cabbage Patch dolls. Also available are fresh-baked tarts and spicy patties. Open Monday through Friday, 9 A.M. to 4:30 P.M.

Index

Fodor's Travel Guides

U.S. Guides

Alaska
Arizona
Boston
California
Cape Cod
The Carolinas & the
  Georgia Coast
The Chesapeake
  Region
Chicago
Colorado
Disney World & the
  Orlando Area

Florida
Hawaii
The Jersey Shore
Las Vegas
Los Angeles
Maui
Miami & the Keys
New England
New Mexico
New Orleans
New York City
New York City
  (Pocket Guide)

New York State
Pacific North Coast
Philadelphia
The Rockies
San Diego
San Francisco
San Francisco
  (Pocket Guide)
The South
Texas
USA
The Upper Great
  Lakes Region

Virgin Islands
Virginia & Maryland
Waikiki
Washington, D.C.

Foreign Guides

Acapulco
Amsterdam
Australia
Austria
The Bahamas
The Bahamas
  (Pocket Guide)
Baja & the Pacific
  Coast Resorts
Barbados
Belgium &
  Luxembourg
Bermuda
Brazil
Budget Europe
Canada
Canada's Atlantic
  Provinces
Cancun, Cozumel,
  Yucatan Peninsula
Caribbean
Central America
China

Eastern Europe
Egypt
Europe
Europe's Great
  Cities
France
Germany
Great Britain
Greece
The Himalayan
  Countries
Holland
Hong Kong
India
Ireland
Israel
Italy
Italy's Great Cities
Jamaica
Japan
Kenya, Tanzania,
  Seychelles
Korea

Lisbon
London
London Companion
London
  (Pocket Guide)
Madrid & Barcelona
Mexico
Mexico City
Montreal &
  Quebec City
Morocco
Munich
New Zealand
Paris
Paris (Pocket Guide)
Portugal
Puerto Rico
  (Pocket Guide)
Rio de Janeiro
Rome
Saint Martin/
  Sint Maarten
Scandinavia

Scandinavian Cities
Scotland
Singapore
South America
South Pacific
Southeast Asia
Soviet Union
Spain
Sweden
Switzerland
Sydney
Thailand
Tokyo
Toronto
Turkey
Vienna
Yugoslavia

Special-Interest Guides

Bed & Breakfast
  Guide to the Mid-
  Atlantic States

Bed & Breakfast
  Guide to New
  England
Cruises & Ports
  of Call

A Shopper's Guide
  to London
Health & Fitness
  Vacations
Shopping in Europe

Skiing in North
  America
Sunday in New York
Touring Europe